Frederick Denison Maurice

Sequel to the Inquiry

Frederick Denison Maurice

Sequel to the Inquiry

ISBN/EAN: 9783744704588

Printed in Europe, USA, Canada, Australia, Japan

Cover: Foto ©ninafisch / pixelio.de

More available books at **www.hansebooks.com**

TO THE INQUIRY,

WHAT IS REVELATION?

IN A

Series of Letters to a Friend;

CONTAINING

A REPLY TO MR. MANSEL'S

"EXAMINATION OF THE REV. F. D. MAURICE'S STRICTURES
ON THE BAMPTON LECTURES OF 1858."

BY THE REV.

FREDERICK DENISON MAURICE, M.A.,

CHAPLAIN OF LINCOLN'S INN.

Cambridge:
MACMILLAN & CO.,
AND 23, HENRIETTA STREET, COVENT GARDEN, LONDON.

1860.

PRINTED BY
JOHN EDWARD TAYLOR, LITTLE QUEEN STREET,
LINCOLN'S INN FIELDS.

SEQUEL TO THE INQUIRY,
WHAT IS REVELATION?

"Now what great and high objects are these, for a rational contemplation to busy itself upon! Heights that scorn the reach of our prospect; and depths in which the tallest reason will never touch the bottom: yet surely the pleasure arising from thence is great and noble; forasmuch as they afford perpetual matter and employment to the inquisitiveness of human reason, and so are large enough for it to take its full scope and range in; which, when it has sucked and drained the utmost of an object, naturally lays it aside, and neglects it as a dry and an empty thing."—*South's Sermons,* vol. i. p. 16.

CONTENTS.

Letters.

Page

I. PURPOSE AND PLAN OF THESE LETTERS.—MR. MANSEL'S AND MR. CHRETIEN'S PAMPHLETS . 1

II. THE DOUBLE SENSE OF WORDS.—TIME; ETERNITY; SELF 7

III. STYLE.—SCHLEIERMACHER.—FANCIED AGREEMENT.—HARD AND PROUD WORDS.—MORAL NEEDS OF OXFORD STUDENTS 26

IV. THE 'TIMES' NEWSPAPER.—THOMAS A KEMPIS. —MR. MANSEL'S TESTS 38

V. THE PRAYER-BOOK.—KNOWLEDGE OF GOD.— AUTHORITIES 53

VI. AN EXAMINATION OF WITNESSES 61

VII. SIR WILLIAM HAMILTON 104

VIII. BUTLER 122

IX. RATIONALISM AND DOGMATISM. — THE TWO METHODS OF ASCERTAINING THE FORCE OF WORDS.—APPEALS TO THE CONSCIENCE, ARE THEY DELUSIVE?—THE VALUE OF QUOTATIONS 135 his character or his piety has any, even the slightest, foundation to rest upon (see seventh Letter). And I would call upon any friend of Mr. Mansel to say whether the charge of having told a wilful lie for the purpose of convicting him of a heresy (see the thirteenth Letter) is supported by evidence upon which he would convict the worst man in England of that or even any less tremendous enormity. Righteous Laymen regard this class of offences with peculiar disgust. They suspect clergymen of an especial tendency to commit them. Knowing that they will be severe and intolerant judges, I wish them to be judges in my case.

The friend to whom these Letters are written was willing that I should publish his name, which would have conferred honour on my book and on me. I have not accepted his kind permission, because I do not wish to make him in the least degree responsible for the opinions which I have expressed, from many of which he may dissent.

London, January, 1860.

SEQUEL TO THE INQUIRY,

WHAT IS REVELATION?

---◆---

LETTER I.

PURPOSE AND PLAN OF THESE LETTERS.—MR. MANSEL'S AND MR. CHRETIEN'S PAMPHLETS.

My dear Sir,

Few persons I think can have studied the controversy between Mr. Mansel and me as carefully as you have done. You have looked at our books with the eyes of a critic and of a layman. In many important points of opinion you differ from me. You have often said that you regretted the vehemence of my language. You have told me very recently that you trusted a grand debate concerning morals and theology would not be degraded into a personal altercation. For all these reasons I have asked that I might address to you any observations which I might wish to make on Mr. Mansel's Examination of my statements. You are aware that he has said in that examination that I have "produced a book which

" for gross misrepresentation, insulting sneers, coarse
" invective, and calumnious imputations, has, as far
" as he is aware, no parallel in the literature of the
" present generation." (*Examination*, p. 100.) He
has said also, you will recollect, that I have uttered "an accusation which is utterly void of truth,
" and which I must have known to be void of truth
" at the moment when I wrote it down." (*Examination*, p. 79.) If these charges are established by sufficient evidence, they must of course exclude me from
all respectable society, and prevent me for ever from
opening my lips as a clergyman. In the effort to
confute them, I might easily be tempted into foolish
and violent protestations; I might forget how very
insignificant a thing my character is in comparison
with the cause in which I am engaged. The recollection that you are my correspondent may, I hope,
save me from this danger. I shall be sure that I am
addressing one who will not start with assuming me
guilty of such enormities; who will at least wish that
I may be able to clear myself of them. And knowing that however friendly you may be, you would
rather believe me the weakest of advocates than suspect the principle for which I am struggling of weakness, I shall try to make every word I say on my
own behalf subordinate to the illustration and vindication of that principle.

I propose to throw my remarks into a series of
Letters, each of which will refer to some subject

that is handled in Mr. Mansel's pamphlet. By taking this course I shall give my readers an opportunity of judging whether I have met or evaded any charge which he has brought against me. I shall be able to explain how, in my judgment, that special charge affects the general issue. I may be obliged to speak more of myself than is agreeable to the reader or to me. But I hope I shall not say anything of my opponent which can appear, even to him, unfairly personal. If I have used any such language in my former book, I shall not be hindered from confessing it by any indignation which his recent accusations have inspired me with.

In this, as in my longer treatise, I shall quote very freely from Mr. Mansel. On that subject of quotations I wish to make a preliminary remark, or rather, an appeal to your experience. You have heard in what respect my Letters are said to be without a parallel in literature. I venture to ask you as a critic extensively acquainted with the controversial writings of our day, whether you know of any in which greater pains were taken that the opponent might speak for himself, not in broken, dislocated sentences, but in connected discourse; not in his weakest passages, but in those which he would himself have selected for extracts? I ask you whether I did not exert myself to the utmost that I might be detected if I was guilty of any misrepresentation of his purpose? I knew it was not enough to implore the reader to consult the original work, though I did implore him frequently. I knew it was not enough to give references. From my own pages he should confound me, if I practised any dishonest arts. I will mention a curious instance of what I mean. The 'Saturday Review' contained an article on 'What is Revelation?' In it I was accused of "ingeniously" omitting, in the very first page of my preface, the adjective 'infinite,' which Mr. Mansel had applied to the nature of God. How did the reviewer know that I had omitted it? *Because the words stood on that very page just as they were taken from the preface to Mr. Mansel's third edition.* Since neither Mr. Mansel nor I had the least doubt that the nature of God is an infinite nature, I repeated, a few lines below, in my language, what he had already said in his. Singular ingenuity! How diligently I must have studied in the Fagan school, where the art of extracting handkerchiefs and epithets is taught!

As I have alluded to a critic who gave me pain, I must refer to a writer who has caused me a livelier and deeper pleasure than I have often known. Mr. Chretien's Letter to me appeared at the same time with Mr. Mansel's answer. I knew that he had devoted earnest attention to the subject. It appears that he has studied my book, as well as Mr. Mansel's, more diligently than perhaps any one except yourself. I am not personally acquainted with him. He is an admirer of Mr. Mansel. He thinks I have often been wrong. His gentleness would dispose him to judge hardly of my impetuosity;

yet he says deliberately that I have attacked my opponent in "no unknightly or unchristian spirit." Such a testimony from a man whose own spirit is so eminently knightly and Christian, is to me of unspeakable value.

I have no wish however to call witnesses to character before I have examined the charges that are alleged against me. It is for no such purpose that I have referred to Mr. Chretien's letter. It strikes me as a curious psychological fact, that two men of the same university, both logicians and scholars, should have arrived at such directly opposite judgments respecting the same volume. The simple and obvious explanation of that fact I take to be this:—There being two possible interpretations of the book and of different passages in it, one of which interpretations would consist with the belief that the writer was indifferently honest, the other of which would convict him of baseness and maliciousness of the worst kind, Mr. Chretien has accepted the first of these as the most probable one, and Mr. Mansel the second.

It will be one object of these Letters to show in reference to each particular allegation in the 'Examination,' that if I might have intended to speak plain words, or to indulge in an insulting sneer, Mr. Mansel has given me credit for the sneer; that if I might have designed to take his words exactly as any one else would take them, or to misrepresent them grossly, he has assumed that I designed to misrepresent them grossly; that if according to one construction of my sentences, I might have spoken truly, and according to another have lied foully, he has thought it necessary to impute the lie. But evidently I ought not to stop at this point. I ought to show that the sense he has put on my words is *not* the obvious one, *not* the one which is most in harmony with the context, *not* the one which would be most consistent with my general purpose. I ought to show next why, without any evil motive such as he attributes to me, he may have accepted the more difficult and less natural version of my words as the most reasonable, extending the well-known canon of criticism, which refers to the readings of a MS., to the printed utterances of an obscure mystic.

In the next Letter I shall illustrate what I have said by an instance. But I trust that I shall do more than that. At the risk of being egotistical, I think I shall be able to show you and my other readers why I have felt so strongly respecting the doctrine and method of the 'Bampton Lectures,' why I have seemed to the lecturer to be assailing not them but him. The remarks which I have to make will lead us into the very heart of the controversy. They are still intended for theological students preparing for Orders and in Orders, though they will not, I trust, be without interest to laymen like yourself.

Very sincerely yours,
F. D. M.

LETTER II.

THE DOUBLE SENSE OF WORDS.—TIME; ETERNITY SELF.

My dear Sir,

You will find the following note at p. 10 of the 'Examination:'—

"I may take this opportunity of warning the reader, once for all, against a favourite expedient of Mr. Maurice's, of which he avails himself in several parts of his work. This consists in seizing upon some expression which his opponent uses in a strictly metaphysical sense, or in a sense specially explained in the place where it occurs, and then assuming the identity of this with some popular sense which he can attack by his usual method of sneer and inuendo. The word *Time* is one of those thus treated. In the 'Bampton Lectures,' *existence in time* means existence in duration and succession, existence continuous but divisible into successive moments, as distinguished from the *nunc stans*, or existence of which every portion is present at once, and from which all successiveness is excluded. In

" this sense, *time* does not necessarily imply that the
" continuous existence ever had a beginning, or will
" ever come to an end. In another sense, *time* is
" used to signify a terminable, as distinguished from
" an everlasting duration; and in this sense the
" *things of time* mean the perishable things of this
" world. Mr. Maurice avails himself of this am-
" biguity to insinuate that his opponent desires to
" fix men's minds on the things that are seen and
" temporal, instead of on those that are unseen and
" eternal. (pp. 103, 352, 428.) *Personality*, or *Self*,
" is another expression which is treated in like man-
" ner. In the 'Bampton Lectures,' it means that
" one permanent individuality which continues un-
" changed through all the various modes of con-
" sciousness, and without which no mode of con-
" sciousness is conceivable by us. In a popular
" sense, *self* means man's earthly desires and enjoy-
" ments, and the thoughts associated with them. Mr.
" Maurice seizes upon a passage where it is used in
" this latter sense, to confute his opponent who uses
" it in the former. Thus he exclaims (p. 378), 'Our
" ' old English poet says,—

" ' Except he can
Above himself erect himself, how poor a thing is man!'

" The moral of the 'Bampton Lectures' is, 'If he
" ' tries, by one means or another, above himself to
" ' erect himself, what a fool is man!' It is chari-
" tably to be hoped that Mr. Maurice never saw the

"context of the lines which he quotes; indeed, he
"gives them so inaccurately that we may fairly sus-
"pect that he knows them only at second-hand. The
"continuation of the passage would have been too
"palpably inapplicable even for his controversial
"license.

> "'And that, unless above himself he can
> Erect himself, how poor a thing is man;
> And how turmoiled they are that level lie
> With earth, and cannot lift themselves from thence,
> And never are at peace with their desires,
> But work beyond their years, and even deny
> Dotage her rest, and hardly will dispense
> With death; that when ability expires
> Desire lives still; so much delight they have
> To carry toil and travail to the grave.'"
>
> (Note, p. 10, *Examination*.)

In a later page, as I have remarked already, Mr. Mansel finds himself "compelled" with "the deepest regret," to charge me with an act of wilful falsehood. But you see from this note that he supposes the habit of falsehood to be formed in me, so that it works naturally, almost of course. I have "a favourite expedient," that is his phrase, of which it is necessary to warn the reader once for all. It is the expedient of confusing together two senses of a word, and imputing that one to a writer which obviously is not his. I have done this with reference to the word *Time*, in order to insinuate that Mr. Mansel "desires to fix "men's minds on the things that are seen and tem-

"poral, instead of on those that are unseen and "eternal." Three pages are quoted from my book which strike Mr. Mansel as having this object, and as illustrating my "usual method of sneer and inu-"endo." I must extract them, that you may judge of them for yourself.

"Such preachers the parables have been to the hum-
"ble and meek, who have asked Christ, as the Disci-
"ples did, to tell them why He spoke by parables,
"and to interpret the parables which they have found
"in every street and alley, as well as in every hill and
"stream. We are told, brethren, that they have been
"deceiving themselves. No real knowledge of the
"Eternal is possible; our conceptions are bounded
"by the finite and the visible. My answer is:—If
"that is the reason, no knowledge of the seen and the
"temporal is possible. Slavery to our conceptions,
"as the teacher of experimental science has shown
"us, is the hindrance to any real, solid acquaintance
"with the mysteries of Nature. When we try to
"bind her with the forms of our intellect, she will
"give us no faithful answers; she will only return
"an echo to our voices. Here is another proof of
"the analogy between things sensible and spiritual.
"The same enemy blocks the entrance into both
"regions. The determination to measure all things
"by ourselves, to bring everything under the con-
"ditions of our intellect, makes us exiles from the
"Kingdom of Heaven and the Kingdom of Earth.

" That determination in other days was called, Pride;
" in ours (words alter their meaning so strangely), it
" claims to be owned as the profoundest humility.
" We dare not presume to burst the shackles which
" God has imposed upon us; we dare not dream of
" ascending above the world in which He has seen
" good to place us; that we do not is the great sign
" that we accept Christianity with childlike submis-
" sion. We prove our allegiance to the Gospel by
" affirming that it is *not* given us to know the mys-
" teries of the Kingdom of Heaven; that the parables
" of Christ are *not* real revelations of it."—(*What is
Revelation? Sermon VI.*)

" He (Mr. Mansel) has taken great pains to show us
" that our finite intellects can never be the measure of
" the Infinite. The maxim is established; it is one to
" start from. And because the finite cannot be the
" measure of the infinite,—because our conceptions
" can never be the measure of that which is,—because
" those conceptions will lead us only to the apparent,
" therefore we need that which shall be the measure
" of our finite thought, which shall lift us above
" our conceptions, which shall bring us into con-
" tact with that which our conceptions are feeling
" after, but cannot reach. He has shown us that a
" mere negation, such as is expressed by the word
" Infinite, can never content a creature who needs
" what is positive, living, personal, to rest upon. We

"heartily sympathize with the observation. For In-
"finite, let us substitute the word which is so dear to
"St. Paul and St. John. Let us speak of the Eter-
"nal. Let us distinguish, with St. Paul, between the
"things that are seen, which are temporal, and the
"things that are not seen, which are eternal. Let us
"speak not of knowing the Infinite, but of knowing
"Him who is from the beginning, Him who was and
"is and is to come. So we shall be in exact harmony
"with the teaching of Scripture; so shall we avoid
"mere speculations about that which is at a distance
"from us; so we shall be brought to ask for that
"which is the ground of our own being; for that
"Rock on which we and the Universe are resting."—
(*What is Revelation?* p. 352.)

"Believing, as our fathers did, that He came to re-
"veal the Eternal God, Him who is, and was, and is
"to come,—believing that He did manifest that life
"of Righteousness, Love, Truth, which is not and
"cannot be limited by Time,—believing that these
"are the invisible things which St. Paul opposes to
"the visible things that are temporal,—believing that
"the Gospel means the admission of men in Christ,
"into the possession and enjoyment of these Eternal
"Treasures, which men in the ages before His coming
"were feeling after, and in which they were sure that
"they had an interest,—believing that to be without
"these Eternal treasures, is to be in the state which

"the Apostles describe as Death, Eternal Death, that
"to possess them in any measure is to have a taste of
"Eternal Life, that to possess them altogether, to live
"and dwell in them, to go no more out of them, to
"sink no more back into our own evil nature, is the
"reward which God has prepared for those that love
"Him, the fullness of joy which is at His right-hand,
"—believing that this is the teaching of the Bible,
"and that the more we read it, the more that teach-
"ing explains to us all the capacities of good as well
"as of evil in ourselves,—I am not afraid of Christ's
"own language."—(*What is Revelation?* p. 428.)

These passages, you will remember, are selected by Mr. Mansel himself. He has given his interpretation of them. Will you listen to mine?

That there are two senses of the words which concern us most,—one metaphysical, one popular,—is a doctrine which most of us are taught, which some of us receive implicitly. Long before I heard Mr. Mansel's name I was forced to ask myself whether I could accept it. I was not then contending with any opponent except myself; I was trying to find a foundation upon which I might stand. It seemed to me that neither of these forms of speech gave me such a foundation, or even helped me to discover it. One told me the opinion about certain great facts which was current among doctors. The other told me the opinion about the same facts which was current among pulpit orators. Was there no way which led directly to the facts themselves? In physics unquestionably there is. The opinions which prevail in the cave and forum, —idols our great experimental teacher calls them,— are thrown down; the things themselves can be investigated and apprehended. Is there no similar method for investigating and apprehending moral truths, those in which man is chiefly interested? When we are occupied with them, are we merely floating in a sea of traditions, or obliged to adopt whatever maxims have established themselves in a particular age?

I had much help from several books in extricating myself from this fearful puzzle. But the Bible was the great help of all. That, I thought, spoke of a substantial, eternal world, in which men were intended to find a home. If what it said was true, the words which described that substantial, eternal world must be most strictly metaphysical words. And yet they must be also most strictly popular words; words for the people, for human beings as such. I found temporal things in the Bible opposed to eternal, but not in the way of contempt or disparagement. The greatest justice was done to both. The world which we see with our eyes was never treated as popular preachers treat it. It had its own honour. It derived honour and grandeur from its associations with the other. The Kingdom of Heaven, the Kingdom of Righteousness, Peace, Truth, was the substantial, the Eternal Kingdom. The more men kept that before them, dwelt in it, the more faithful they would be to the business of the changeable, visible world; the more worth they would attach to all its transactions.

Using this guide, it seemed to me that I could look straight at the words which concerned us most, such as Time and Eternity; that I need not give either two senses; provided I looked upon the permanent as the standard for the changeable and fleeting, and did not attempt to deduce the nature of the higher from that of the lower. I fancied the Scripture language, instead of shrinking into a little corner of its own, and declining all comparison with any other, was capable of being tested by the metaphysical inquiries and beliefs of all peoples and ages. I could not doubt that it was, at the same time, the popular language, that it would go straight home to the very heart and spirit of our people—of the poor, to whom the Gospel was first preached—because it addressed itself, not to that which is superficial and accidental, but to that which is deepest in all, and common to all.

These convictions were working in me long before I took Orders in the English Church. They were the result of many personal conflicts, and of intercourse, limited enough certainly, but lying chiefly among young men of stirring and active minds in the Universities and in London. When I did take Orders, my sphere of work was not among them, but amongst the inmates of a hospital. I felt myself as ignorant as a man could well be of their wants and feelings; as afraid as any one could be, that I should talk of things which had no interest for them, or which they could not understand. I was sure I should do this if I fell into either the scholastical or what is called the popular style; if I either discoursed to them about the beauty of virtue and the mischief of vice, or, on the other hand, urged them to abandon thoughts of their bodies for thoughts of their souls, when God, by His visitation, had compelled them to think of their bodies, and of what they were suffering in them, and when their benevolent medical friends were doing their utmost to relieve their bodily sufferings. But I could not forget that at the Universities we are trained in what are there called Humane studies. It seemed to me, that if I had profited as I ought to have done by those studies, I should be able to address men, not in a university dialect, not in the dialect of a stump orator, but in a human dialect. I had *not* profited as I ought by those studies; therefore my success was very imperfect. But so far as I connected my humane education with the divine lore of Scripture, and tried by that means to make amends for my defects, so far I felt that I could speak to men with nothing of what we call culture,—with only *that* culture which is obtained from suffering and sorrow and the sin which was often the cause of both. And this because I could tell them of an Eternal

Being of absolute goodness and truth, whom they were created to trust and to know; and who, that they might trust Him and know Him, had revealed Himself in One who had borne their sickness and sorrows and sins; because I could tell them, that by trusting in Him who was the same yesterday, today, and for ever, they might be delivered from their sins, might rise above themselves and their own bad nature. I repeat it; I found I could make some of these men understand me. And if I have in later years ever succeeded in making any men who *have* culture understand me, it has been from following the same course; from assuming that they had that in them which was craving for the Eternal and the Infinite, even as they had that in them which led them to turn away from it, and dwell wholly in the changeable and the transitory; and from endeavouring to show them that they could never deal bravely and manfully with changeable and transitory things, or pay them the reverence to which they have a right, while they raised them into gods; that they could see the earth and all its beauty clearly, and love it heartily, while they walked in the light of the heavenly sun which is looking down upon it.

Now, if you will do me the favour to read over the passages in my book to which Mr. Mansel has alluded, I think you will judge that they *might* have been written by a person who did not resort to the expedient of confounding two distinct senses of the word 'time' for the sake of blackening an opponent's character. They might express a very strong and deep conviction which made such an "expedient" absolutely impossible, such an object preposterous. And if you will then turn to Mr. Mansel's comment on these passages, you will perceive that this *must* be the interpretation of them, and that the other cannot be. For (1) the idea of Eternity as opposed to Time in these passages is precisely that which Mr. Mansel attacked me for holding six years ago. (2) That idea of Eternity is incompatible with either of the definitions of Time which he supposes that I am trying to confound. (3) It is especially incompatible with that definition upon which he supposes me to ground my insinuation against him of "desiring to " fix men's minds on the things that are seen and " temporal." (4) You must be aware—if Mr. Mansel is not—that my doctrine upon this subject is one which makes me specially unpopular with the religious world, and that his has made him peculiarly popular. An expedient for raising a prejudice against him on this ground would therefore seem about the absurdest and most hopeless that ever entered into a human brain.

But in spite of these startling and obvious presumptions against Mr. Mansel's interpretation of my words and my purpose, I am satisfied that it appeared to him the only possible one. It could not be otherwise. He allows all varieties of opinion among those who accept the double sense of words, and who are content to receive his two definitions of Time. Those who try to break down the barrier between the metaphysical and the popular regions,—those who refuse to deduce Eternity from Time at all,—are simply unintelligible to him. He does not mean to be unjust to them, but as he cannot account for their vagaries, he must, whenever they come into contact with him, give them credit for some dark design. He cannot believe that they are really as stupid as they pretend to be. They *must* accept his definition, though they say they do not. And if they do, and yet maintain their own ground, I can see as little as he can that there is any escape for them from the guilt of direct inconsistency, insincerity, and falsehood.

Mr. Chretien has not imputed to me the 'expedient' or the villanous purpose which is involved in it, because, as it seems to me, he *is* able to understand something of the processes of mind which have led me to reject the double sense of words and to seek for a meaning of Eternity which does not make it a mere extension or a mere negation of Time. He carefully guards himself against being supposed to adopt my method or to approve of it. But he has, if I am not mistaken, felt most bitterly the perils of the double sense of words. The remarks upon his own sufferings when he heard Mr. Mansel's Lectures, in pp. 33-36, expressed as they are with the greatest modesty,— with profound respect to the talent of the Lecturer and thorough confidence in the goodness of his intentions,—have done much to confirm me in my conviction on this subject, and to assure me that a number of earnest and thoughtful men who would be most inclined by their intellectual discipline to arrive at an opposite conclusion, must be passing through the struggles which I passed through, and must be feeling their way to a similar result.

At the same time it cannot escape you or any observer of our times, that both in the schools and in the world theirs is a struggle against a prevailing habit, one into which we are all apt to fall, one which is eagerly adopted and recognized as a right one by the guides of opinion in both regions. The moment Mr. Mansel's Lectures appeared, they were welcomed by a great part of the religious press of the country as *the* academical defence of Christian truths. Such a recognition of a book which was in its nature scholastic by the unscholastic world, I do not think any of us have witnessed in our time. You may imagine how such a phenomenon must have struck a person strongly persuaded that the schools and the world ought to be mutual helpers, but equally persuaded that each may do incalculable injury to the other, and that this injury is no way so likely to be effected as by the uncertainty whether the words of preachers are to be taken scholastically or popularly, and by the opportunity which the admission of a double sense affords of giving them one force or another, as they may answer best to refute an unbeliever or a heretic. You will understand, I think, how that confusion which Mr. Mansel attributes to me, may have been the effect which I most feared from the publication of his Lectures,—how his acknowledged metaphysical ability may have made me dread more than I can at all express their effect upon those who are not metaphysicians, as well as upon those who are. That this dread may have often betrayed me into heat of language, that the difference of our habits of mind may have caused me to misunderstand him as he has misunderstood me, is quite possible. Whenever I discover that to be the case, I trust I shall not be slow to confess it.

Nay, I will go a little further. In a somewhat excited passage (p. 85), in which he scarcely preserves his usual tone of conscious and lofty superiority to his antagonist, Mr. Mansel intimates that I have laid down one law for his conduct and another for my own. I will show you by an instance how far this is the case, and on what maxims I desire that we should respectively be judged. If I shall find that I have anywhere charged him with resorting to an expedient for perverting and confusing the meaning of words that he might injure the character of any one of the eminent men whom he has attacked in his Lectures or his Notes, I shall not offer any of the explanations for myself which I have felt that I ought to offer for him; I shall simply say that I had no business to suspect a man of probity of such an intention, and that I beg his pardon for having been tempted to suspect him.

After this remark, I shall not make any parade of candour in owning at once, as I ought to own, that I made a gross blunder in quoting from Daniell. It is no sufficient justification, that I wrote the letter which contained that quotation in the country, where I had not access to books; for I could easily have corrected it afterwards, and ought to have done so. The folly of having made a ten-syllable line into a bad Alexandrine, and of having substituted *except* for *unless*, I fully admit. I am thankful to undergo the exposure for such carelessness; I am thankful also to Mr. Mansel for quoting the whole passage from which I had taken a line and a half. He is right in his conjecture that I did learn that line and a half at second-hand more than thirty years ago, and that it has remained in my memory without any thought about the surrounding sentences. If I do not mistake, I found it first in the note or preface to one of Mr. Wordsworth's poems. I believe I received it along with his interpretation of it, which may not be the true one since it differs from Mr. Mansel's. Nothing which I see in the whole passage in the least proves to me that it was not the true one. Daniell *may* no doubt have meant merely what the dullest preacher would mean, when he talks of those

> "That level lie
> With earth."

Or he *may* have meant to explain why they so lie, and why they cannot lift themselves up. Rightly or wrongly I supposed (with my betters) that he did mean this. At all events I found in his words a very beautiful hint as to the reason which kept *me* on this level. I found that I had in myself that which aspired to rise above its own level and that which was content to stay upon its own level. The one I learnt from St. Paul to call the spirit, the other the flesh. I learnt also from him that it was possible to live after the flesh and so to die, or to live after the spirit, and so to enter into fellowship with those eternal things which eye hath not seen, nor ear heard, nor hath it entered into the heart of man to conceive. Having adopted this nomenclature, I was less disposed here even than in the other case to give that strictly metaphysical sense to the word *self,* according to which " it means that one " permanent individuality which continues unchanged " through all the various modes of consciousness, and " without which no mode of consciousness is conceiv- " able by us," or that " popular sense" in which it " means man's earthly desires and enjoyments, and " the thoughts associated with them." These definitions are exceedingly well; but where am *I ?* I, the person, am lost in that grand personality. I, who have the desires and enjoyments and thoughts, am confounded with them. The more I converse with people of any class or school whose minds are exercised with questionings or doubts, the more do I perceive them writhing under these formulas, utterly unable to connect them with their actual experiences and sufferings. To such I can make myself intelligible so long as I do not desert St. Paul's method for any conceit of my own. But I am too well aware how often those conceits intrude themselves and mar the effect of that which in itself I believe to be the right and divine way of speaking to one's fellow-men and fellow-sinners. Chiefly to that cause—though partly to their habit of resolving each person into a personality (just as our modern political writers reduce Nations into Nationalities)—I attribute it that I always have been, and I fear always must be a barbarian, and worse than a barbarian, to eminent scholastic teachers like Mr. Mansel, as well as to the whole body of popular critics, High Church, Low Church, Broad Church, Orthodox, Unitarian, Calvinistical, Freethinking, who assume a certain scheme of opinion, and by *that* measure and judge the Universe. They do and must suppose that when I profess to speak of the evil in myself, I am hinting at the evil which is in some one else, and am consequently indulging in "insulting sneers;" that when I declare my belief in a good which is within the reach of us all, and which I know best by the reproaches of my conscience for not having attained it, I am boasting of my superiority to other men; that when I talk of an Infinite Charity, which I need to fill up the hollowness in myself, and to overcome my tendencies to bitterness and hatred, I wish people to give me credit for possessing that charity.

I am not afraid that those who know me and my ordinary manner of teaching will fix *these* charges upon me. But that Mr. Mansel should attribute to me almost immeasurable cant and hypocrisy, ought to cause me no sort of surprise. I rather wonder that, looking at me from his point of view, he has been able to find words strong enough for the expression of his disgust and scorn. If he is right, the method into which I have been led is utterly and hopelessly wrong. That I have made it appear so to any who might have benefited by it is cause for serious repentance. But I do not believe that even a wise man could have caused it to look reasonable or tolerable in the eyes of the Bampton Lecturer.

Ever very truly yours,
F. D. M.

LETTER III.

STYLE.—SCHLEIERMACHER.—FANCIED AGREEMENT.
—HARD AND PROUD WORDS.—MORAL NEEDS OF
OXFORD STUDENTS.

My dear Sir,

You may think that I was unreasonably diffuse in my comments upon the Note which I considered in my last Letter. But in it you will find the key to all my differences with Mr. Mansel, to the censures in every other part of his pamphlet, to the relation between the personal question about which few can be interested but ourselves, and the moral one in which all mankind is interested. My present Letter will be chiefly occupied with matters of much less importance. At page 4 of the pamphlet you will find these words:—
" To some indeed of Mr. Maurice's charges I shall not
" attempt to reply at all. I do not think it worth
" while to enter upon a controversy in defence of
" the merely literary character of my Lectures. Mr.
" Maurice, in his anxiety to leave no weapon of attack
" unemployed, has discovered that my style is in one
" place ' bewildering,' in another ' jargon,' in another

"'a wilderness of words,' in another 'vagueness,' in
"another 'slipslop' (whatever that may mean); and
"that my thoughts exhibit 'terms and realities hope-
"lessly mingled.' I am quite ready to plead guilty to
"these charges, if my accuser's writings are to be con-
"sidered as examples of the opposite qualities. I will-
"ingly admit that my notions of clearness of thought
"and accuracy of language are diametrically opposed
"to his." (*Examination*, p. 4.) A very kind writer in
the last number of 'Fraser's Magazine' has made the
following remark upon this passage :—"Who has not
"presented to him here the picture of one who, deter-
"mined seriously to wound, is glad to envenom the
"wound with as much superfluous outrage as may be?
"Now, will it be believed that scarcely one of the pas-
"sages in Mr. Maurice's book, to which we are referred
"—and as Mr. Mansel gives us references, every reader
"can try the experiment for himself—partakes of the
"quality of literary criticism, criticism on style, in
"the ordinary sense of these words? A particular
"phrase, not necessarily viewed as Mr. Mansel's in-
"vention or peculiar property, is contrasted with liv-
"ing reality as 'school jargon.' With no mention of
"style at all, it is complained that a point which Mr.
"Maurice considered essential to the argument is left
"in 'vagueness.' So much for two of the alleged
"grievances. The rest we can leave to the reader
"who will follow our example of verification." I am
particularly grateful for this comment upon the words,

and will try the process of verification which the Reviewer recommends in the other cases. The charge of "bewildering" is this:—"The observations re-"specting Creation with which this passage closes, "seem to show that Mr. Mansel had a sense of this "earlier order, otherwise they would be out of place. "They are bewildering, will prove more and more be-"wildering, to the consciences of his readers, will "darken all practical principles to them, will make "action as impossible as belief, so long as we revile "other persons for rejecting the plain words of Scrip-"ture, and refuse to accept these words as the guides "of our own thoughts." I do not see what criticism upon an author would be possible, if one was not at liberty to remark that some of his words were in this sense bewildering, or how such a remark can possibly be construed into a general attack upon Mr. Mansel's style, or into a resolution to "leave no weapon of at-"tack unemployed." I did say (p. 320) that I wished Mr. Mansel "had not rushed into a wilderness of "words about the combination of the One and the "Many." Whether the passage I referred to deserves to be called a wilderness of words or not, the reader may judge for himself. At all events the charge concerned the matter of the argument; only the style so far as it bore upon the matter. The slipslop phrase to which I objected was one in which Mr. Mansel spoke of "views in their essential features." It certainly struck me that this was a phrase which one might rather have expected to meet in a speech of Lord Castlereagh's than in the discourse of an accomplished Oxford scholar. It is the single instance, I believe, in which I have complained of the language for its own sake. The complaint would have had no force if it had not applied to an author from whose general character and talent such a solecism was *not* to have been expected, one who had been generally and deservedly praised for his command of language. That I spoke of terms and realities being hopelessly mingled in a great part of the Lectures, is strictly true. It is an objection to the character and substance of them, to the very principle which they are written to maintain. No change of style could have made a difference in this respect; oftentimes the confusion of which I speak becomes more evident to the reader from the transparency of the mere form in which it is exhibited.

I have answered these charges in detail. Now look at the whole passage as it stands, and ask yourself whether a writer who accumulates points of evidence of this kind, and founds such a conclusion upon them, might not very readily persuade himself that I had " produced a book which for gross misrepresentation, " insulting sneers, coarse invectives, has no parallel in " the literature of the present generation."

In the note to p. 5 are these words:—" He objects " to my attributing to Schleiermacher a theory con- " cerning Religion, because the original is *Frömmig-*

"*keit,* which ought not to be translated Religion." Will you kindly turn to p. 315 of my book? I have written there:—"Now I think any one who "will be at the pains to refer to the 'Christliche "Glaube' of Schleiermacher, will discover that he "certainly was not putting forth a theory on the "subject of Religion or of Prayer. Rightly or "wrongly, he had evidently a dread of theories in "this region. He was disposed, his opponents al- "ways say, to exaggerate the feeling above the intel- "lect." To the word *Religion,* in the first of these sentences, I subjoined a note, of which this is the first line: "*Frömmigkeit* is his word, which, I submit, "ought not to be translated Religion." Now it must surely be evident to any one who reads this passage, with the pages which follow it, that the emphatic word in the sentence to which the note was subjoined, is not *Religion* but *Theory.* The observation about the translation in the note, was merely an accidental and subsidiary one. What I am complaining of Mr. Mansel is, that he imputes to Schleiermacher an elaborate theory about Religion, when the characteristic of his mind was, that he exalted personal consciousness or feeling above theories. It was desirable for this purpose to remark, that *Piety* was the exact translation of his word. It was all the more important, *because* he identified Piety with Religion. I wished the reader to observe that he did, and therefore that Mr. Mansel's attempt to reduce his account of Religion into a theory, however ingenious, was necessarily a misrepresentation of his object. Had Mr. Mansel, in the least degree, apprehended this purpose, he would see that the elaborate attempts to confute me in the note, have either no bearing upon the point which I raised, or are confirmations of my remark. But this is just one of the cases in which, as I have shown you already, it is impossible that he can apprehend those who differ from him. He must make them theorists, whether they like it or no. He cannot contemplate them or their thoughts till he has fixed them in a theory. The method which Schleiermacher had learnt in his laborious study of the Platonic Dialogues, was just, I conceive, that which he was trying to apply in his theological inquiries. This was the link between the Herrnhutter and the Philosopher. That method of rising by questionings of common facts into the perception of eternal realities, Mr. Mansel, of course, cannot recognize. To interpret Socrates, he must turn him into a theorist, just as he has turned Schleiermacher into a theorist. Whatever in his discourses could not be brought within these limits, he would agree, with the old Comedian, in ascribing to the inspiration of the Cloud-Goddesses, and would assume to belong to the mysteries of their worship.

The other misstatement which Mr. Mansel notices, I am glad at once to correct. I had rashly spoken in my preface of Mr. Mansel having intimated a hope that we were essentially agreed in opinion. I omitted, he says, the qualifying words, "on this "question, at least." And he adds, "I was neither "so sanguine nor so simple as to cherish any belief "in a general agreement between Mr. Maurice's the-"ology and mine." My object was simply to thank him for his courtesy, and to express my fear, that even on the question to which he alludes, about the meaning of Scripture, I was not in agreement with him. But he is fully entitled (he will, I am sure, exercise the right) to withdraw that passage and every passage which can be construed into even a partial approval of any word that I have ever written on theology or any other subject. Have I not a right also to demand that he will strike out those sentences in his Examination which express "respect" for the character of one whom he has accused of deliberate falsehood? Can such words be sincere in him? Must they not be most offensive to me?

With two more of these miscellaneous charges I will conclude a Letter which it is disagreeable for me to write and for you to read. They are contained in pp. 16–18 of the Examination.

"The rest of Mr. Maurice's first Letter is devoted "to vituperation instead of argument, and may safely "be left to stand or fall by its own merits. He consi-"ders the Bampton Lectures to be full of 'hard and "'proud words spoken against those who were crying "'out for Truth.' Other critics have expressed a very

" different opinion of the spirit in which that work is
" written. One of the most antagonistic of its re-
" viewers (excepting, of course, Mr. Maurice himself),
" while pointing out two instances, and two only,
" which he considers exceptions (and even one of these
" is an error of his own), admits that 'the general
" 'spirit of the book is scholarly and liberal; and pro-
" 'bably the deviations from this tone are involun-
" 'tary and intellectual merely.' Another critic as-
" serts that the author 'displays great liberality, not
" 'only as regards persons but questions;' while a
" third speaks of the 'true courtesy with which he
" 'has treated those from whom he has most differed.'
" Mr. Maurice, of course, is welcome to hold a differ-
" ent opinion; and indeed, to judge by his own wri-
" tings, he seems to have adopted a somewhat peculiar
" standard of literary courtesy. The following speci-
" men belongs to the present Letter: we shall come
" to more hereafter. 'A man,' says Mr. Maurice,
" 'may grovel in the sty without attracting any spe-
" 'cial notice from the modern defender of Christi-
" 'anity; if he aspires by an irregular method after
" 'righteousness, no laughter is too loud for his pu-
" 'nishment.'

"I shall leave it to the readers of the Bampton
" Lectures to judge for themselves, whether the argu-
" ment of that work required, or even admitted, any
" 'special notice' of 'men who grovel in the sty;' or
" whether the method employed in dealing with the

D

"intellectual errors which it professes to notice is that
"of 'loud laughter.' I quote the passage only as a
"specimen of Mr. Maurice's notions of fair and cour-
"teous controversy, and as an edifying contrast to the
"'hard and proud words' which he has discovered in
"the Bampton Lectures."—(*Examination*, pp. 16–18.)

As I had not a perfectly distinct recollection of my own words, I really believed on Mr. Mansel's authority that I had said that the Bampton Lectures were full of "hard and proud words against those who were "crying out for Truth." Will you let me repeat to you what I did say?

"He who holds that the Bible testifies from its first
"page to its last that God has created men for the
"knowledge of Himself, and is kindling in them a
"thirst for that knowledge, a discontent with anything
"which comes short of it,—cannot by possibility lis-
"ten without the profoundest interest to every cry of
"men after it in one age or another. He must not
"ask first what they have failed to attain, but what
"they have been permitted to attain. He must be
"glad to learn from their blunders as well as their
"successes: perceiving in the first the likeness of his
"own; in the second, the guidance of God. He may
"not expect their opinions or conclusions to do
"much for him; their struggles and questionings and
"glimpses of light he will cherish, and be thank-
"ful for. All will appear to him to be pointing to a
"full-orbed Truth which is not in them but in God,

" and which He has manifested in the Eternal Word,
" the only-begotten Son. The remembrance of hard
" and proud words spoken against those who were
" crying out for Truth will be always the bitterest in
" his life, that which recurs to him with the keenest
" sense of having grieved the Holy Spirit of God, of
" having brought upon him the curse of a brother's
" blood."—(*What is Revelation?* pp. 142, 143.)

Now I should have thought any one who read this passage must have perceived that I *could* not be referring in it to Mr. Mansel; that I must be referring to Mr. Mansel's opponent. What those remembrances are to which I alluded, it is not necessary that I should state to you or to any man. That I am the only person who could make the discovery, were it demanded, the only person I had in my mind when I put the words on paper, the Searcher of hearts knows. What words may not be turned into an "insulting sneer" if it is assumed that these form one?

The other sentence about the class of persons who were and were not attacked by " modern defenders of Christianity" was not intended specially for Mr. Mansel. It was less applicable, I thought, on the whole, to him, than to some of those whose sentiments he has adopted, and whose apologies he has lauded in his notes. I do not know that, except in his treatment of Hegel and Marheinecke, in the fifth Lecture, he has used language which out of a church would have provoked "loud laughter;" whereas it is apparently the habitual purpose of one author especially for whom he has expressed much respect, to produce either that ebullition against all doubters and unbelievers,— often men of high aims and purposes, however much they may be in error,—or else that settled scorn which certainly is not better for those against whom it is directed or for those who indulge it. But I did consider, and do consider, that the complaint occurs fittingly in an answer to the Bampton Lecturer. He is the able and popular champion of a regulative morality against a speculative or absolute morality. He was addressing a body of young men, one out of a hundred of whom might be tempted to worship Hegel, every one of whom might be tempted to break through the laws of ordinary morality; to think basely of the female sex, and to forget the duties which men owe to them; to bribe at elections; to gamble and run into debt; to make money his object and his god. Was this no opportunity for the regulative moralist to prove his superiority to the speculative or absolute moralists? Could he not have turned their empty impracticable suggestions into contempt, by showing how *his* bore upon the life and conduct of those who sat around him, or who would read his lectures afterwards?

A Lecturer, with this purpose before him, with these prodigious advantages for effecting it, appeals to the reader " whether the argument of his book re-
" quired or even admitted any special notice of those

"who grovel in the sty." Be it so. Then on behalf of English parents I implore University Lecturers and Preachers to choose arguments which *do* require and admit such notice. And if they shall discover that they cannot hinder our children from falling into the sty, or raise them out of it, unless they set forth the Eternal and the Infinite Being as actually revealing Himself to our race, that the members of it may actually apprehend Him, and so be delivered from their own grovelling tendencies, I trust that no theories which they have heard on that subject, no evidence of the exceeding popularity of the theorist in the religious world, will hinder them from giving the help to practical morality which the whole country demands at their hands.

Very truly yours,
F. D. M.

LETTER IV.

THE 'TIMES' NEWSPAPER.—THOMAS A KEMPIS.— MR. MANSEL'S TESTS.

"In his first Letter," says Mr. Mansel, "Mr. Maurice opens the attack by an insinuation that the teaching of the Bampton Lectures is destructive of all contemplative piety. To support this charge he avails himself of a criticism published in the 'Times' newspaper, the writer of which mentions the following inference as one *which many minds will draw* :—
'All mystic Theology disappears before this doctrine at once. The followers of Thomas à Kempis, in all their degrees, the whole list of religious men who have endeavoured to abstract themselves from sense and its conditions, are proved the merest triflers.'*

---

* "This extract from the 'Times,' which is here given verbatim, and only alluded to by Mr. Maurice, furnishes a good instance of my antagonist's fairness in quotation. The writer of the above criticism immediately adds, 'We do not expect Mr. Mansel to admit these probable consequences of his theory, or to accept them as legitimate consequences at all. We call attention to them as inferences which many minds will draw from his theory, *whether le-*

" Mr. Maurice of course accepts the inference, and " exclaims, 'Am I quite prepared, were that all, to " ' part with the Imitation of Christ, the most che-" ' rished book of devotion throughout Christendom, " ' dear to Romanists, to Protestants, to Quakers,— " ' the companion of the sick in hospitals, of the soli-" ' tary prisoner?' "—(*Examination*, pp. 6, 7.)

As I spoke of the article in the 'Times' from recollection, I feared when I read this note that I had done the writer and the Lecturer serious injustice. With some trembling I procured the number for the 11th of January. I will give " verbatim " a much longer passage than Mr. Mansel has given :—

" Divines have been accustomed to suppose that " the region of higher truth is peculiarly their own. " They have soared in imagination above merely phe-" nomenal existence, and contemplated the purest " forms of being. They have discoursed of the In-" finite and Eternal, without any suspicion that they " were using words without ideas. To cross the limits " of space and time has been with them a matter of " everyday adventure. Beyond the limits of the visi-" ble and sensible world they have sought the point

" ' *gitimately or not.*' This statement in Mr. Maurice's hands assumes " the following form :—' He pointed out, with the skill and conscien-" ' tiousness of a logician, certain results which *followed inevitably* " ' from Mr. Mansel's doctrine.' The ' skill of a logician' is a quality " for which Mr. Maurice generally professes very little respect : the " above sentence almost warrants a suspicion that his contempt ex-" tends to the ' conscientiousness' also."

" of view from which they might perceive its real pro-
" portions, and set a proper value on the temporal
" and finite. Eternity, they have exclaimed, is more
" than time,—infinity, something greater than the
" realms of space can hold. Mr. Mansel's argument
" will make those of the race uncomfortable who sur-
" vive to hear it. Eternity, they have to learn, is the
" absence of time; Infinity, the negation of space.
" Till we can escape from these positive conditions of
" thought, we must remain in ignorance of their mys-
" terious negatives. Imaginable, the world has long
" known that they are not. Imagination, if it is more
" active than thought, can travel a less distance. We
" cannot paint to the mind's eye a polygon of a thou-
" sand sides, though we can conceive it, and may even
" know that it exists. We cannot imagine, though
" we can conceive, the depths to which the Atlantic
" cable is sunk, or the long succession of miles through
" which it stretches from continent to continent. But
" Infinity and Eternity, according to Mr. Mansel's
" doctrine, are neither imaginable nor conceivable. If
" so, what are the words but signs without a thing
" signified,—symbols with no conceptions to answer
" to them? What are the propositions into which
" they enter but verbal juggles without sense or mean-
" ing? At best, the strength and force of the nega-
" tive concept must vary with that of the positive.
" The more fully our minds are occupied with time
" and space, the more closely we can approach to their

"contraries. The finite thus becomes the only school
"in which we can study the Infinite, and the distinct
"appreciation of the temporal is the best proximate
"measure of the Eternal. All mystic Theology dis-
"appears before this doctrine at once. The followers
"of Thomas à Kempis, in all their degrees, the whole
"list of religious men who have endeavoured to ab-
"stract themselves from sense and its conditions, are
"proved the merest triflers. Their minds, removed
"from outward objects, could rise to no higher reali-
"ties, but were forced by the law of their being to
"contemplate either nothing or themselves. But we
"must not confine our thoughts to a single religious
"school, or even to religion at all. How does the
"glory depart from art, and the inner light from
"nature, its lesson from the rolling ocean, and their
"moral from the everlasting hills; how much worse
"than idle become all the strivings of the soul after
"a pure and elevated ideal, if, in the endeavour to
"rise above the earth, it can but dash itself against a
"heaven of iron, and when it seeks an object of love
"and worship, finds but a negation!

"When Rationalism and Mysticism are gone, dog-
"matic Theology must follow. It is useless, though
"it is possible, to construct syllogisms and affect for-
"mal demonstrations when dealing with unconceiv-
"able terms and unmeaning propositions. Some of
"the orthodox divines whom Mr. Mansel would most
"approve are essentially deductive. Some truths, the

"first principles of theological science, they gained, as
"they supposed, from reason, and some from Revela-
"tion. Here was a sure basis on which to erect with
"anxious care and thought a temple of eternal veri-
"ties. Vain aspiration! The statue must fall from
"its pedestal, for iron is mixed with the clay. Re-
"velation addresses us through our faculties, and
"Reason is one of our faculties; and our faculties
"can tell us nothing of the Absolute and the Infinite,
"which they can neither know or conceive. Our
"conclusions cannot contain more than our premises.
"No logic can extract positive truth from negations.
"Turn over your selected propositions as often as you
"please, and arrange them as best you may, you can
"extract nothing from the mind which is not pre-
"viously in it; and your supposed objective Theology
"will be but a reflection of yourself.

"We do not expect Mr. Mansel to admit these pro-
"bable consequences of his theory, or to accept them
"as legitimate consequences at all. We call attention
"to them as inferences which many minds will draw
"from his theory, whether legitimately or not."

Now I think the reader of this eloquent passage, which I have preserved in its original order, will arrive at conclusions not very different from these.

(1) That I did great injustice to my cause in merely referring to a single clause of it. (2) That the paragraphs before the qualifying sentence leave a far stronger impression of the inevitable conse-

quence of Mr. Mansel's statement than my meagre allusion to Thomas à Kempis can have conveyed. (3) That this qualifying sentence does not efface the impression, but only suggests the thought that Mr. Mansel may see an escape from the apparently inevitable conclusions, which the reviewer does not see. (4) That this qualifying sentence does not follow "immediately" on the passages respecting Thomas à Kempis, but after a long intervening paragraph respecting dogmatic theology. (5) That the writer might very naturally not expect Mr. Mansel to acquiesce in what he said about dogmatic theology, and might expect him to assent to any inferences which were fatal to Rationalism and Mysticism, in the last of which classes the followers of Thomas à Kempis would be generally reckoned. (6) That no person of ordinary candour can possibly suppose Mr. Mansel to have used the word "immediately"—though it affects very seriously the meaning of the Article—from "contempt of conscientiousness," or from any cause but the carelessness to which all writers are liable. I do not know whether it will be considered a point in my favour,—any evidence that I have not unlawfully strained the purpose of the writer in the 'Times,'— that Mr. Chretien does not mention that among the instances in which I have dealt unfairly with my opponent. Perhaps he is not as well acquainted with the criticism as Mr. Mansel.

The really important question however is, whether

those "many minds" were right, which, on the lowest rendering of the reviewer's words, would think that Mr. Mansel's statement proved "the followers of "Thomas à Kempis, in all their degrees," to be the "merest triflers." The writer in the 'Times' explains the feeling of these many minds by saying that, according to Mr. Mansel, "the Finite becomes the "only school in which we can study the Infinite, and "the distinct appreciation of the Temporal is the best "proximate measure of the Eternal." Mr. Mansel observes, "The mysticism of à Kempis, a very subor- "dinate feature in his work, is of a practical, not a "speculative character." Whether subordinate or not, the remark that it is essentially practical is undoubtedly true. The "many minds" would care nothing for Thomas à Kempis were it otherwise; the sick in hospitals and the solitary prisoner must be very indifferent to any Mysticism that is not practical. I endeavoured to reconcile the instinct of these many with the reason which the critic assigned, by observing that a Divine Teacher of man's spirit, with whom he could converse, was assumed throughout the 'Imitation of Christ,' that this was the characteristic of the book as a practical book, that this had endeared it to practical and suffering people. I had no occasion surely to support this assertion by extracts. Every one who has looked into the 'Imitation,' who knows the form in which it is cast, must be aware that it ceases to exist as a manual of devotion, that all its words lose their significance, if the "disciple" in the fourteenth century and in all subsequent centuries might not as much hold converse with Christ as those who sat with Him in the ship on the sea of Galilee, or walked with Him in the streets of Jerusalem. In other words, the idea of the book is that there is an Eternal Teacher ever near to the disciple, who is endeavouring to draw him away from "sense and its "conditions." And it certainly did seem to me, as to one of the many, that if the Infinite could be only approached through the Finite, the Eternal through the Temporal, this postulate of à Kempis was an utterly false one. To this objection Mr. Mansel makes answer:—

"In the preface to the Bampton Lectures, the in-
"quiry which that work is intended to pursue is stated
"as follows:—' Does there exist in the human mind
"' any direct faculty of religious knowledge, by which,
"' in its speculative exercise, we are enabled to decide,
"' independently of all external Revelation, what is
"' the true nature of God, and the manner in which
"' He must manifest Himself to the world; and
"' by which, in its critical exercise, we are entitled
"' authoritatively to decide for or against the claims
"' of any professed Revelation, as containing a true
"' or a false representation of the Divine Nature and
"' Attributes?' The reasons for answering this
"question in the negative are given in the third Lec-
"ture, in which it is maintained that the Infinite,

"as such, is not a direct object of human know-
"ledge, on account of certain limitations to which
"all human thought is subject. The limitations spe-
"cified are four in number, which may be briefly
" enunciated as follows:—(1) There must be an
"object about which to think; and this object must
"be distinguishable from other objects. (2) There
"must be a person to think; and this thinker
"must be distinguishable from the object about
"which he thinks. (3) There must be a time to
"think in; and this must have a certain limited
"duration, as a portion of the life of the thinker, and
"must succeed or precede other portions of time, in
"which he is thinking of other objects. (4) Attri-
"butes of body must be conceived as existing in
"space; and attributes of mind as existing in a person.
" No mode of knowledge which does not profess to be
"exempt from one of these four conditions is repudi-
"ated by the Bampton Lectures, as 'impossible in the
"'very nature of things.' "—(*Examination*, pp. 9–11.)

Now, in the statement of this question, there are four or five words the meaning of which cannot be taken for granted, upon which in fact the whole controversy turns. What is meant by "a faculty of "religious knowledge"? What is meant by its "speculative exercise"? What is meant by "external "Revelation"? What is meant by deciding "inde-"pendently" of external Revelation? It was exactly because I thought that every one of these expressions required to be sifted before any propositions which were grounded upon them could be of the least worth, that I wrote my Letters. If "a direct faculty of reli-"gious knowledge" means a faculty of knowing the Being in whom we live and move, as a child knows its father, then I think that such a knowledge is implied in the 'Imitation of Christ,' and in all writings of the same character, nay, more or less in all devotional writings whatsoever. If, on the other hand, by "direct faculty of religious knowledge," is meant a faculty by which the child *comprehends* the Father, the Finite the Infinite, most persons, of all schools, would *in terms* repel so monstrous a notion; while all of us are liable to fall into it, because all of us are tempted continually to make ourselves gods. The question is surely open, whether the evil is ever corrected in us till we discover that we have a divine faculty which will always be likely to put forth extravagant pretensions when it is denied its legitimate functions. If, again, by the "speculative exercise" of this faculty, is meant the exercise of looking out beyond the limits of the finite and the visible, beyond itself, this too, I think, is the assumption of such writers as à Kempis, and more or less distinctly the assumption of all devotional writers whatsoever. If, on the other hand, by "speculative" exercise is meant, as in the former case, that the speculation embraces within its terms and limits that which, by the hypothesis, is transcendent and infinite, I should say again that no school or sect ought to be charged, except on the clearest evidence, with admitting so huge a contradiction; but that there does seem a great danger of those approaching the very edge of it, who think that Man has no faculty which raises him above the terms and limits of his own understanding, and who yet confess an Infinite and Eternal God, whom he is in some way to approach and (not ignorantly) to worship. So, thirdly, if by "external Revelation" is meant the unveiling and discovering to Man by God Himself of His own Nature and Character, I apprehend that Thomas à Kempis and all his followers would say, that this is the revelation or unveiling which the Bible speaks of, and that we cannot, consistently with the acceptance of the Bible, deny that God has created men with faculties to receive such a revelation; that it is, in fact, the ground of all their discoveries, the means by which all their powers are awakened. If, on the other hand, any have said that men's faculties could be awakened without *such* an external revelation, or that without it they have any faculties which could judge of the nature of God, I think it should be carefully inquired whether these opinions are not attributed to many who do not actually hold them; and whether those who do, or think they do, may not have been led into their opinion by statements which seem to imply that men have no faculties whatever for receiving such a Revelation, or apprehending from whom it came, or whether it contain a true or a false representation of the Divine Nature and Attributes. These are the questions which are at issue. You will see, I think, how easy it is, by the use of certain words, such as Religious, Knowledge, Revelation, to lose all sight of the principles which they involve. When, therefore, Mr. Mansel says, in reference to the passage which I have extracted, " By these tests the Lectures may " fairly be tried in reference to any school of theolo- " gians which they are supposed to approve or to " condemn," I demur to the statement altogether. I maintain that every one of these tests must be tested again before one can the least understand whom it does or does not approve or condemn. And I think that the instinct of the " many minds," which leads them with satisfaction or with sorrow to confess, that all the theologians to whom the 'Times' reviewer refers, or to whom I refer, must be sacrificed, if Mr. Mansel's positions are maintained, is a sound instinct, and one which will endure much severer tests than those which Mr. Mansel has applied to his Lectures.

The assertion that such books as Thomas à Kempis must be "sacrificed" or "expelled from libraries" if Mr. Mansel's opinions are adopted, which was made in my Letters, and which I have repeated now, has created much surprise and contempt in his mind. I would gladly withdraw such expressions, if on reflec-

E

tion they appeared to me exaggerated. I cannot feel that they are. Manuals of devotion which have become associated with the highest delights and the severest conflicts of those who use them, when they are discovered to proceed upon a false principle, cannot be treated like a history or an astronomical lecture, which has been superseded by later information and a more expanded science. A bitter moral disappointment, a sense that the writer has helped us to deceive ourselves about questions in which deception is most serious and terrible, will make any half-measures in this case impossible. Those who have seen these cruel reactions—those who have felt them—will understand me.

But Mr. Mansel goes on:—" Let it be granted that "this or that writer (mystic or not) has so far de- "ceived himself as to mistake for a divine revelation "what is in reality but the result of his own medita- "tions;—still those meditations may be pious and "profitable, though we regard them as the work of a "human author, possessing no supernatural safeguard "against human errors, and having no title to be be- "lieved as articles of the faith. It may suit Mr. "Maurice's purpose to confound these two questions, "as it suited him, in his 'Theological Essays,' to "identify the inspiration of Holy Scripture with the "inspiration of religious men. The majority of his "readers and mine, with the Sixth Article of the "Church of England to assist them, will probably be "able to distinguish between the two."—(*Examination*, pp. 13, 14.)

I am very glad that Mr. Mansel is able, by help of the Sixth Article, to settle the question about the limits of Inspiration to his own satisfaction. As I do not find the word Inspiration once used in that Article, I should have been thankful if he would have told me how I was to cure my errors on the subject by its teaching. The Sixth Article tells us what are the Canonical books of Scripture, and what are the Apocryphal. I acknowledge the Canonical as Canonical, and the Apocryphal as Apocryphal. If the Church had required me to hold a certain theory about the absence of Inspiration in the Apocryphal books, or in any other books, I suppose she would have told me so; there could not certainly have been a more convenient opportunity. As to the presence of Inspiration in the writers of the Canonical books, I think I accept it in at least as full a sense as Mr. Mansel does. The extreme horror which I feel of the theory of Dictation, arises from a belief, right or wrong, that it is wholly at war with the idea of Inspiration; that holy men could not speak as they were moved by the Holy Ghost if they put down certain letters mechanically; if they acted as amanuenses, not as men.

Some may deem Mr. Mansel's allusion to my 'Theological Essays' not relevant to the question in hand. I differ from them. I am grateful to him for introducing it, not only because it gives me an opportunity of making a remark upon the Sixth Article which I believe may relieve some minds of a great embarrassment, but because the question respecting Thomas à Kempis and the Mystical Writers may receive some illustration from that remark. Should any one attempt to establish an Article of Faith out of Thomas à Kempis, or out of any book which I have a greater reverence for than I have for his, I should offer as stout a resistance as my opponent. But that these writers, or any writers who have expressed any deep truth or exercised any good moral influence over the world, were merely uttering their own meditations, were not under the guidance and teaching of God's Holy Spirit, this I am not prepared to concede, precisely because I *do* accept those Canonical books of Holy Scripture, precisely because I *do* learn my Articles of Faith from them. Those Articles which are included in the third portion of our Creed, those which most emphatically belong to the New Testament, are grounded, as I hold, on a manifestation of the Holy Spirit, as the Inspirer of all right thoughts, good counsels, and just works. To say that where I find these, the inspiration of God's Spirit is wanting, is, in my judgment, to set at nought the testimony, not of the Apocryphal, but of the Canonical books.

Very truly yours,
F. D. M.

LETTER V.

THE PRAYER-BOOK.—KNOWLEDGE OF GOD.—AUTHORITIES.

In Mr. Chretien's Letter to me (p. 15) I find the following words:—

"At the beginning of the fifth Lecture, we find Mr.
"Mansel expressly recognizing the knowledge of God
"as possible, and speaking of it as ' a consciousness
"' of the relation of a Person to a Person' (p. 143).
"The *sense* of these words recurs continually in this
"and the preceding Lecture; I select them because
"they are perhaps those in which Mr. Mansel gives
"his belief on this subject the simplest and most
"quotable expression. Surely, Sir, they are worthy
"grave attention. They must remove from your
"mind the suspicion which you entertained (p. 139),
"that the Lecturer must tremble at the thought of
"our using such phrases as these—'We who know
"' Thee now by faith'—'In knowledge of Whom stand-
"' eth our eternal life.' To accept phrases like these,
"when they occur in our Liturgy or elsewhere, is as
"easy for Mr. Mansel as for you or for myself.

"Whatever differences there are between you (and they are neither few nor unimportant), this, at least, is not among the number. On one common ground you meet,—'This is life eternal; that they might know thee, the only true God, and Jesus Christ, whom thou hast sent' (John xvii. 3)."

This admonition, so kindly and truthfully expressed, has reference to a remark which I made in my first Letter respecting the alterations in the Prayer-book which will be necessary if the doctrine of the Bampton Lectures was established. I cannot say how heartily I thank Mr. Chretien for it. I did certainly think that the accusation against Schleiermacher in the 16th note to Mr. Mansel's fourth Lecture justified me in applying a somewhat severe rule to himself respecting that which might constitute hypocrisy in the act of prayer. But if I left the apprehension upon a mind so open and honest as Mr. Chretien's, that I was judging Mr. Mansel, or fancying that he used a prayer which he must use habitually, in a less real or devout sense than I used it myself, I desire at once to withdraw the expression. It was intrinsically wrong; it was especially inconsistent with all my professions; for I have always declared that I believed acts of prayer to be those in which men rise above themselves and all their dogmatic confusions, so that the prayers of divines should never be measured by their arguments or opinions, and that they themselves should be tried by the former rather than by the latter. To have lost sight of this principle in speaking of any person, would be a far greater sorrow to me than to have incurred any of Mr. Mansel's denunciations. Without justifying the fault, I will explain how I fell into it. I was writing, as Mr. Chretien supposes, not to a single theological student only, but to a whole class of theological students, with whom, directly or indirectly, I have been in contact, whose difficulties and dangers I have known. To make them afraid of saying that the words they use when they are praying for and with their people only mean so and so; to convince them that they mean more, not less, than they mean when they are used in the ordinary intercourse of life, and that prayer itself is to teach them how *much* they mean,—this has been, and I trust always will be, a principal object with me whenever I am trying to influence this class. Now I cannot help feeling every day that such teaching as Mr. Mansel's, however little it may interfere with his own apprehension of this Collect, must lead and is leading numbers to take it in a non-natural sense; perhaps I should rather say, is justifying them in the very inadequate and unreal sense which they give to it already. The astonishment which I have seen expressed in various journals, Church and Dissenting, at my notion that the words of St. John, which Mr. Chretien has quoted, do really point to a knowledge of God in the strict sense of the words,—their evident feeling that Mr. Mansel's sense is the strict one, and that the Bible's is a rhetorical or metaphorical one,—confirms me in the dread which I indicated. I believe, in my heart, that those words in the Prayer-book are the great protection against the opinion that we cannot know the Infinite and Eternal God; and that while we heartily pray them, no double senses of the word 'know' will ever establish their dominion over us.

This was what I meant by referring to the Collects. Certainly the last thing that was in my mind was to indulge in "sarcasm" against Mr. Mansel. I was writing very earnestly on behalf of myself and of a multitude of other men. I knew nothing of him as an individual; I merely felt about him as a writer who had put forth a doctrine which had met with great acceptance, and which it seemed to me would have more effect in undermining the lessons I had learnt in the Prayer-book,—lessons I believe we all require to be deepened in our hearts,—than any which had been circulated by any professed enemy of our Church. I cannot change that opinion. But Mr. Mansel says:

"Mr. Maurice, if he has honestly read the book
" he is criticizing, must be perfectly well aware that
" the application of this argument is not limited to
" the Bampton Lecturer. He must have found, in
" the notes to that book, quotations from writers of
" various ages and countries, some of them at least
" of unimpeachable orthodoxy,—Fathers, Greek and
" Latin, mediæval and modern Divines, Philosophers,

" Englishmen, Frenchmen, Germans,—all concurring
" in the confession, that the Infinite is beyond the
" reach of man's reason; that the absolute essence of
" God is unknown; that the Divine attributes are
" apprehended, not directly in themselves, but indi-
" rectly in their relations to us. The following, to
" say nothing of more questionable authorities,—
" Justin Martyr, Theophilus of Antioch, Clement of
" Alexandria, Athanasius, Basil, Gregory of Nyssa,
" Cyril of Jerusalem, Augustine, Anselm, Aquinas,
" Hooker, Bramhall, Cudworth, South, Browne,
" Berkeley, Butler, Whately, Hampden, Lee, Des-
" cartes, Pascal, Bartholmèss, Leibnitz, Jacobi, Storr,
" Neander, Drobisch, form a goodly array of divines
" and philosophers, every one of whom, if Mr. Mau-
" rice's judgment is trustworthy, would have 'trem-
" bled' at using the Collect for the Epiphany and
" the second Collect at Morning Prayer. Of these
" I shall repeat but one quotation, which has already
" been given at length at the close of the third Lec-
" ture, and in that position could hardly have been
" overlooked by any moderately attentive reader.
" The writer from whom it is taken is one not ge-
" nerally supposed to be peculiarly hostile to the
" doctrines and services of the Church of England.
" ' Dangerous it were for the feeble brain of man to
" ' wade far into the doings of the Most High, whom
" ' although to know be life, and joy to make men-
" ' tion of his name, yet our soundest knowledge is

"'to know that we know him not as indeed he is, "'neither can know him; and our safest eloquence "'concerning him is our silence, when we confess "'without confession that his glory is inexplicable, "'his greatness above our capacity and reach.' In "such company I am quite content to bear my share "of Mr. Maurice's sarcasm; and notwithstanding his "lucid dissertation on the word *know*, and his denun- "ciation of the 'confused and unsatisfactory' charac- "ter of those discourses which do not employ the "term in his sense, I venture to assert once more, as "I have asserted before, that knowledge by faith is "not knowledge by sight or by demonstration; and "that a knowledge which is sufficient for the pur- "poses of religious life and worship, may be insuffi- "cient for the purposes of a Speculative Theology."
—(*Examination*, pp. 14, 15, and 16.)

I certainly did not enter in my former volume into an examination of the authorities enumerated in this extract. I will make amends for the fault in this Sequel. In the next Letter I will consider them one by one, omitting those who are still alive in our own land. In general I shall not be content with merely looking at the passages which are given in Mr. Mansel's notes, though I will do my best to discover their sense as they stand. I will also inquire whether they do not gain fresh force from their context, and from the general purpose of the writers. I do not promise to accept their statements, whatever they may be, as controlling the language either of the Bible or the Prayer-book. But I shall be most thankful to discover what they do say; whether they confirm Mr. Mansel's belief respecting the Infinite and Eternal; whether they contradict my belief as to the objects of Revelation. One author, of greatest worth and weight, I shall not have need to quote in his chronological place. I quite agree with Mr. Mansel, that the passage he took from Hooker could " not " have been overlooked by any moderately attentive " reader of the Lectures." I at least did not overlook it. I referred to it in these words:—

" Mr. Mansel quotes a beautiful passage from " Hooker in this Lecture, one from Augustine in " the next, both of which indicate what deep awe " they had of the Being in whom they were living " and moving and having their being; how, as one " worthy to stand beside them, our holy and admir- " able Leighton, expresses it, 'The posts of the door " ' of the spiritual temple moved at the voice of Him " ' that cried.' Such passages might have been mul- " tiplied indefinitely; none would have been more " to the purpose than the well-known soliloquy in " the fifth book of Hooker respecting the Eucharist. " They should be read and re-read, that we may feel " how true the saying is, that 'those who know most " ' of God, and trust most in His love, will fear Him " ' most;' how impossible it is to cultivate the fear " of God in any sense in which the Scriptures speak

" of it, if we regard Him as a distant, unknown
" Being, whose Nature and Character we cannot
" enter into, or partake of; how certainly, if we en-
" tertain that opinion, our fear will be taught us by
" the precepts of men; how certainly it will alternate
" between the sentiment of slaves towards a cruel
" Taskmaster, and that of idolaters who have made
" their own Gods, and therefore feel—as the Greeks
" did about their heroes, as the Italians do about
" their saints—that they have a right to scold them
" and scoff at them; how truly the words of Job
" express the whole difference between the mere tra-
" ditional homage, and that which comes from actual
" discovery. '*I have heard of Thee by the hearing
" 'of the ear, but now my eye seeth Thee.* WHERE-
" 'FORE *I abhor myself, and repent in dust and
" 'ashes.*'"—(*What is Revelation?* pp. 352, 353.)

I beg you to remember those words when you peruse the passages from Fathers, Schoolmen, French
and English divines, which will come under our notice
immediately.

Very truly yours,
F. D. M.

LETTER VI.

AN EXAMINATION OF WITNESSES.

My dear Sir,

Mr. Mansel's first reference (Lecture IV., Note 19) is to the sixth chapter of the second Apology of Justin Martyr. It is to this effect, that "the words "Father and Creator, and Lord and Master, are not, "properly speaking, names, but titles or appellations "derived from benefits and acts." It must be difficult, I think, for a reader knowing only these words, to give them a very definite sense. What goes before, makes Justin's purpose intelligible. He is speaking of the Dæmons or Demigods of the heathen mythology. These he derives from that union of the sons of God with the daughters of men, which is spoken of in the Book of Genesis. Each angelic parent, he supposes, gave a name (*e. g.* Poseidon or Pluto) to his offspring. But the Father of all, he says, had no name, inasmuch as he who bestows a name must be older than he on whom it is bestowed. Then follows Mr. Mansel's extract. After which Justin proceeds to speak of Him who alone he truly called Son, the

Word, who was ever with the Father, being begotten before all creatures. He explains why the name Christ belongs to Him, and how He is to overcome the Dæmons. Doubtless a passage from which much may be learnt respecting the belief of the second century, and which may also be valuable for other reasons. But how it serves Mr. Mansel's cause, or what light it throws upon the question in what sense the words "knowing God" are used in the Prayer-book, I must leave the reader to guess.

THEOPHILUS OF ANTIOCH follows next (Lecture IV., Note 18). It is to this effect, that *as the soul in a man is not seen, being invisible to men, but is discovered through the movement of the body, so likewise may it be impossible that God should be seen by human eyes, though He is discerned through His Providence and His works.* A very suitable and excellent argument as addressed to a heathen like Autolycus, but how it affects those who never dreamed of seeing God with their eyes, who entertain the profoundest horror of idolatry, I cannot imagine.

The next passage (Lecture IV., Note 23) is more astonishing. It is taken from the fifth book of the 'Stromata' of CLEMENS OF ALEXANDRIA. Now, most readers of ecclesiastical history are aware, that Clemens delighted to be called a true Gnostic, precisely because he sought to confute the Gnosticism of Basilides, Valentinus, and others, not, as Tertullian did, by merely denouncing *their* method of attaining to the knowledge of God, but by showing that there is a method of arriving at the knowledge through the guidance and teaching of the Divine and "Philanthropic" Word. The fifth book of the 'Stromata,' from which the extract in question is taken, begins with the clearest and strongest assertion respecting this γνῶσις. Take some of the early sentences of the first chapter.

Neither is Faith without Knowledge, nor Knowledge without Faith. For the Father is not without the Son; in so far forth as He is a Father, He is Father of a Son. And the Son is the true Teacher concerning the Father. And that one may believe in the Son, it is necessary to know the Father, to whom the Son is related. And again, that we may have a knowledge of the Father (ἵνα τὸν Πατέρα προγνῶμεν), *it is necessary to be a believer in the Son, seeing the Son of God teaches of Him. For from Faith to Knowledge; through the Son to the Father. But Knowledge is of the Father and the Son, according to the Gnostical canon (I mean Gnostical in the true sense), the grasping at and apprehending* (ἐπιβολὴ καὶ διάληψις) *of Truth is through the Truth.*

In the chapter of this book from which the extract in the note comes, Clemens has ascended to the very sublime of this Alexandrian doctrine. He has been speaking of the Greek Mysteries as indicating the truth, that purification is the step to the highest knowledge. The greater Mysteries, he says, have no longer reference to learning, but to the actual contemplation of Nature and things in themselves. Then pointing out how, by confession and the other acts of the Christian life, this Pagan doctrine may be turned to its truest sense, he talks of arriving, after having abstracted the soul from all bodily desires, at the Monad or Unity; then how this is to be disengaged from all notions of position or locality. The sentence Mr. Mansel has quoted follows, wherein he exhorts, that throwing aside " whatsoever appertains " to bodies, or to the things that are called incorpo- " real, we should cast ourselves into the greatness of " Christ, and thence go on by a process of holiness " into the Immeasurable, and so should come to the " knowledge of the Omnipotent, not however as if " we could take measure of that which it is, but " rather of that which it is not." On this last clause, of course, the whole stress of Mr. Mansel's quotation rests. Whether it can rest safely there, after the passages to which I have referred, and the hints which I have given respecting the whole life and purpose of Clemens, others may judge. I suspect that the negative knowledge which Clemens seems to affirm as the highest attainable, is explained in the following sentence, wherein he intimates that 'figure and motion and place, and right hand and left,' all of which are connected with God in Scripture, are to be thrown aside by the Gnostic, not as if they were not necessary steps to his knowledge, but as being hints of that which he is afterwards to attain in its simpler essence. The idea of this negative knowledge runs through all writings of this class. It reappears in the fourteenth century in Eckart; Gerson handles it; Mr. Vaughan and Mr. Mansel would say, and say rightly, I conceive, that it reaches its full development in Hegel. In all its forms I feel far more dread of it than sympathy with it. But surely the indication of it in Clemens does not make this passage exactly the authority to which Mr. Mansel should appeal.

The next authority is ATHANASIUS (Lecture IV., Note 18). I will give Mr. Mansel's passage as it stands. "For ofttimes the artist, though not seen, "is known from his works; and just as they say "about the image-maker Phidias, that his productions, "by their symmetry and the proportion of their parts "to each other, show forth Phidias, though not there, "to the beholders; so may we fitly know from the "order of this world the God who is the Maker and "Fashioner of it, even though by the eyes of the body "He is not perceived." What I said about Theophilus, applies emphatically to this passage of Athanasius. He is writing against idolaters and about idolatry. His whole argument has reference to the degradation which Heathens suffer from fancying God to be in the likeness of the objects which are presented

F

to their senses. He had been arguing in the previous chapter, that having immortal souls which they cannot see, they make guesses about God from the things they do see. He had asked them why, as they turned away from God, they do not turn to Him. For they can do this, he says, if they wash themselves from the filth of their lust, and so casting off what is the foreign accident of the soul, will exhibit only that which comes forth from the Creator, that so with it they may behold the Word of the Father, after which they were at first created. He repeats the same sentiment in fuller and more striking language, affirming, "that "the pure part of the soul being thoroughly pene- "trated with light, beholds as in a glass the Word "that is the Image of the Father, and in Him reason- "ably apprehends the Father (τὸν Πατέρα λογίζε- "ται), of whom the Saviour is the Image. Or if the "instruction that cometh from the soul is not self- "sufficing by reason of the things without it that are "disturbing the reason, and because it cannot of itself "see that which is nobler, it is possible again, even from "the things that appear, to lay hold of the knowledge "concerning God; the creation, as in written characters, "through its order and harmony signifying and pro- "claiming its Master and Creator. For God being "good and philanthropic, and caring for the souls that "are placed under Him, seeing that He is unseen and "incomprehensible in nature, being above all created "substance, and seeing that on this account the human

"race would have missed the knowledge concerning
"Him, in that it is formed out of the things that are
"not, and He is without beginning,—for this reason
"God so fashioned His creation by His own Word,
"that whereas He is by nature unseen, He might even
"from the works be made known to men." And then
follow the words Mr. Mansel has quoted. I venture
to ask whether this passage favours more than the
others his doctrine, so far as that is opposed to mine?
Athanasius believed undoubtedly that the creature
cannot by its own efforts ascend to the Creator. That
is the doctrine of my whole book. He contends that
the Creator reveals Himself to the creature, that
it is the proof of His goodness that He does. He nowhere hints that this Revelation is not of what God
is, but "how He wills that we should think of Him
"in our present finite state." This is *the* question.
Do not let us lose sight of it.

BASIL and GREGORY OF NYSSA are Mr. Mansel's next
authorities (Lecture IV., Note 19). I join them together, because the passages which he has extracted are
taken from treatises written by the respective authors
against Eunomius. The object of Eunomius was to
refute the belief of the Church respecting the Generation of the Son, by proving that the idea of generation was imcompatible with the idea of Godhead.
He assumed the epithet ungenerated ($\dot{a}\gamma\acute{e}\nu\nu\eta\tau$ος) to
be *the* epithet for the Divine nature. He would not

admit it to be merely *an* epithet, or to be deduced from human notions. It denoted, or rather, connoted, the Divine substance. To speak of a generated Being as consubstantial with the ὁ ἀγέννητος is a contradiction. The first book of Basil and the twelfth Oration of Gregory are chiefly occupied with arguments on *this* point. There is much of course in both which is not argument but vehement denunciation. Basil especially is provoked, by some allusion of his antagonist to privative or negative words, into the exclamation that he has got that lore from the categories of the pagan Aristotle, with which the doctrine of the Church ought never to be mixed. Omitting however these and other accessories of Basil's discourse, it is an ingenious effort (more able, I think, than the corresponding one of the other Father) to show that Eunomius has bewildered himself by confounding a phrase which expresses just as much as any other phrase a notion *about* the Divine substance, with that substance. The name, "the Unbegotten," Basil contends, can no more represent the nature of God than any other name. Taken by itself, it does not satisfy the human mind; nay, it is derived from the idea of generation; it is merely the negation of that. And then having confuted this very awkward experiment for getting at a Substance which must be above all our notions, through one of these notions, or rather by a denial of one of them, he goes on to say, in the words which Mr. Mansel has quoted, that " the very supposition of

"having found out the substance of the God who is
"over all, what self-conceit and arrogance it is! Let
"us examine him, whence he says that he has come
"into the perception of it. Is it from the common
"judgment of Mankind? That indeed suggests to us
"the existence of God, not what that existence is."
And therefore, Basil goes on to show how, since these
experiments at arriving at the substance of God are
so vain and impossible, since they are found to terminate at last in some notion which we have abstracted,
or in some mere denial of that which is human, God
has manifested Himself in the Only-Begotten Son, who
could truly say, "He that hath seen Me hath seen the
"Father." The whole argument tends to this point.
There must be an Only-Begotten Son to reveal the
Father. There is no contradiction in such a revelation. No doubt Basil believed that in one sense substance—the substance of the earth, the substance of
man, the substance of God—is incognizable. That is
to say, he believed that there is in each person and
in each thing that which constitutes the person or
the thing, the very self of him or it. *That* must be
incommunicable. But the whole end of his treatise is to show that the Son does show forth the perfect image, the exact form of this substance. According to Eunomius, that was impossible; the Unbegotten could not be presented in the Begotten.
What then was Basil, what was Gregory of Nyssa
setting forth, but that very idea of a Revelation of

the real and true God, as He is, in the Person of the Incarnate Word, which I opposed to the idea that God only tells us what "He wills that we should "think of Him in our present finite state"? I cannot be too glad that Mr. Mansel has given us this passage from Basil. It is worthy of the most careful meditation, not only for its own sake, but as the key to the mind of the doctors of the Nicene age generally on the subject of Revelation.

———

CYRIL OF JERUSALEM is referred to in the same note. A very different man, I need not remind you, from Basil or Gregory, a man with much more simplicity of heart than subtlety of intellect, a man who could never enter into the Homoousion of the Council, and yet to whom the greatest champions of that Council have not denied the title of orthodox. Most consistently with this character does he say in the chapter of his Catecheses which refers to the one God, "For we do not declare what is God; but that we "cannot arrive at an exact knowledge about Him, with "humbleness we confess. For in things concerning "God, it is great knowledge to confess ignorance." A beautiful sentiment, and one which I believe most persons whom Mr. Mansel has attacked in his Lectures, would in the best moments of their lives recognize to be no less true than beautiful. It is in strict harmony with the passage from Hooker, and explains, I think, better than almost any we can find, in what

LETTER VI. 71

sense many devout men have, sometimes, seemed to cut off human beings from that knowledge which, in their most fervent exhortations, they were urging them to seek; how earnestly they have confessed ignorance as the very road to Knowledge; how readily they have acquiesced in darkness respecting the *plans* of God, because they have believed that He has revealed Christ's Infinite Goodness and Wisdom in which they can repose.

AUGUSTINE follows next (Lecture V., Note 18). The passage is taken from the thirteenth book of the Confessions. I will use the translation which is given in the 'Library of the Fathers':—" For altogether as "Thou art, Thou only knowest who art unchangeably "and knowest unchangeably and willest unchange- "ably. And thy Essence knoweth and willeth un- "changeably; and thy Knowledge is and willeth un- "changeably; and thy Will is and knoweth unchange- "ably. Nor seemeth it right in thine eyes that as "the unchangeable light knoweth itself, so should it "be known by the thing enlightened and changeable." Did any one ever suppose that the creature knows the Creator as the Creator knows Himself? But hear the end of the passage, which Mr. Mansel has *not* given. " Therefore is my soul like a land where no "water is, because as it cannot of itself enlighten "itself, so can it not of itself satisfy itself. For so is "the fountain of life with Thee, like as in Thy light "we shall see light." Evidently here, as throughout the Confessions, the unchangeableness of God is not a negation of the changeable, but the very ground of all changeable things; the thought and belief of it alone makes them endurable. Augustine can find his rest nowhere but in the Infinite and the Eternal. The whole book is a prayer to be drawn into it; a prayer that God would "satisfy" the soul with Himself since nothing else can satisfy its infinite desires.

ANSELM is named next (Lecture VI., Note 12). The passage selected is from the sixth chapter of his work, 'De Fide Trinitatis.' Anselm is dealing with that tendency to Tritheism which was so prevalent in his time. He says that the mistake which persons commit on this subject, arises from their assuming the necessary separation of human creatures as their starting-point, and arguing that there must be a corresponding separation in the nature of God. Then he says, in the words which Mr. Mansel has quoted, "But if he de-
"nies that Three can be spoken of One and One of
"Three, that the Three cannot be spoken of each
"other mutually, as we do in the three Persons and
"the one God; if he says that because he does not see
"this in other things, neither can he understand it in
"God, let him suppose, just for a moment, that there
"is something in God which his intellect cannot pene-
"trate; nor let him compare a nature which is above
"all, free from all law of place and time and composi-

"tion of parts, with things that are enclosed in place "and time, or are composed of parts. But let him be- "lieve that there is something in that which cannot be "in these, and let him acquiesce in the authority of "Christendom, not dispute against it." Does it not strike Mr. Mansel that this passage cuts two ways, and that the edge which is turned towards him is much the sharper? Is not the Archbishop protesting against the doctrine attributed by the 'Times' Reviewer to the Bampton Lecturer, "that the Finite is "the only school in which we can study the Infinite, "and that the distinct appreciation of the Temporal is "the best proximate measure of the Eternal"?

AQUINAS succeeds Anselm (Lecture VI., Note 17). The passage selected is contained in the 'Summa Theologiæ,' P. 1, Qu. xxxii., art. 1. It contains the conclusion upon a question which has been, as usual, considered first on both sides. The question is this: Can we arrive at any knowledge of the Trinity by natural Reason? The arguments *pro* are derived from the supposed hints of the doctrine in pagan authors, and from those analogies of nature which the Fathers were so fond of observing. *Contra*, there is the assurance of orthodox authorities that the doctrine is especially of the New Testament, and is cognizable only by faith. In the passage which Mr. Mansel quotes, Aquinas decides for the negative, drawing a distinction which the Lecturer considers highly valuable, especially for the confutation of those who would enlist the Neo-Platonist divines among the champions of the Trinity, that by "natural reason those things may be known concern-"ing God which pertain to the Unity of Essence, but "not those which pertain to the distinction of persons." Before Aquinas winds up his article he answers the apparently plausible arguments for the opinion which he has rejected, maintaining that a truth once known may be corroborated by evidence which could never have caused it to be received.

How these statements affect my assertion respecting a knowledge which is derived to us from Revelation and not by independent exercises of the reasoning faculties,—how they at all confute the opinion that we can know Him who reveals Himself, —I do not perceive. Instead of advancing further than Mr. Mansel or Thomas Aquinas in putting forth claims for a knowledge of the Trinity on behalf of the natural Reason, I cannot go nearly so far. The distinction which has been proclaimed to be of such great worth, fails, I think, utterly, when it is referred to the test of History. Have men arrived by natural Reason at the Unity of the Essence? Is not the proclamation, "The Lord our God is one God," in the judgment of most Christians, a special proclamation of God to the Israelites,—that which separated them from the other nations of the earth? And how could this distinction apply to the Neo-Platonists, who notoriously regarded the discovery of Unity as the last and highest discovery of all, that which only the most exalted Philosophers, probably with the aid of mystical rites, could attain? If we hold that God was gradually educating men to the apprehension and knowledge of His own Nature, we may reconcile that first revelation of His own distinction from all creatures with the final revelation of the Unity of the Father and Son in one Spirit; we may believe that that offers the highest satisfaction to the spirit of Man which craves equally for distinction and for oneness. And then the *second* distinction of Aquinas between the light which either Nature or the History of men's thoughts and opinions can *give*, and that which they *receive* when the light has fallen upon them from above, will be of exceeding value. But while we set up Revelation against Reason instead of regarding the first as God's discovery of Himself to the other, we shall be in the double peril of degrading the Reason, and of giving it an unfair and dangerous exaltation.

Passing over Hooker, of whom I have spoken already, BRAMHALL is the next authority to whom Mr. Mansel appeals (Lecture III., Note 3). To see how far his authority bears upon the question, I will simply quote Mr. Mansel's own words.

" This distinction plays a part in the controversy " between Bramhall and Hobbes, the former of whom " says, 'The nearer that anything comes to the es- " 'sence of God, the more remote it is from our ap-

"'prehension. But shall we therefore make poten-
"'tialities, and successive duration, and former and
"'latter, or a part without a part (as they say), to be
"'in God? Because we are not able to understand
"'clearly the Divine perfection, we must not there-
"'fore attribute any imperfection to Him.' To this
" Hobbes replies, 'Nor do I understand what deroga-
"'tion it can be to the divine perfection, to attribute
"'to it potentiality, that is, in English, power.' 'By
"'*potentiality*,' retorts Bramhall, 'he understandeth
"'power or might; others understand possibility
"'or indetermination. Is not he likely to confute
"'the Schoolmen to good purpose?' Hobbes con-
"cludes by saying, 'There is no such word as poten-
"'tiality in the Scriptures, nor in any author of the
"'Latin tongue. It is found only in School divinity,
"'as a word of art, or rather as a word of craft, to
"'amaze and puzzle the laity.' This charge may
"be answered in the words of Trendelenburg. 'In
"'explicandis his notionibus, ex ipso philosophiæ se-
"'cessu depromtis, Latinæ linguæ in philosophicis et
"'laxa remissio et læva inopia in angustias quasdam
"'nos rediget, ut perspicuitatis gratia ad scholasticos
"'terminos confugiendum sit.'"—(*Bampton Lectures*,
p. 327.)

Here no doubt is a valuable discussion about words between two able and accomplished disputants. Mr. Mansel may be very right in taking Bramhall's part against Hobbes on the propriety of using the phrase 'potentiality,' and not identifying it with 'power.' But can any one affirm from this passage that Bramhall belongs to "the goodly array of Divines and Philosophers" who agree with Mr. Mansel's doctrine and reject mine? Surely I am not more disposed than he is to make "Potentialities" and "Successive Duration" and "Former and Latter" into a part of God! It is from this very danger that I am flying when I speak of His Eternity as not being explained by duration. I admit that the nearer anything comes to the Essence of God, the more remote it must be from our apprehension; only I have contended, as I think Bramhall would have contended, that what was far off was brought nigh to us in Christ; that though no man or no angel can ascend into the pure Essence of God, we may with our spiritual eyes behold the very God of very God in Him who was made Man.

In Lecture III., Note 2, SOUTH is introduced to us. The passage is taken from his animadversions upon Sherlock. It recalls to us that melancholy controversy which ought to stand as a perpetual warning to Clergymen who are engaging, as I am, in a controversy about great and holy subjects, how they allow themselves to follow abler and better men, whose wit and wisdom they cannot reach, in their bitterness and personality. While accusing Sherlock of worshiping three Gods, South was betrayed into an audacity and irreverence of jesting which I think must make all men shudder; the more if they feel how easily they might be tempted into the same fault were they conscious of the same gift. Such a recollection, I think, should make us a little cautious how we follow implicitly his statements in this treatise, at all events without balancing them against those that are to be found in his practical Discourses. Subject to this remark, I am most willing that the reader should peruse the following passage, which, if the words *comprehend* and *know* were identical, would seem to me reasonable enough :—

"The second reason of our short and imperfect no-
"tions of the Deity is, *the Infinity* of it. For this we
"must observe, That we can perfectly know and com-
"prehend nothing, but as it is represented to us un-
"der some certain Bounds and Limitations. . . . Upon
"which account, what a loss must we needs be at, in
"understanding or knowing the Divine Nature, when
"the very way of our knowing seems to carry in it
"something opposite to the thing known. For the
"way of knowing is by defining, limiting, and deter-
"mining; and the thing known is that of which there
"neither are nor can be any Bounds, Limits, Defini-
"tions, or Determinations."—(*Bampton Lectures*, p. 326.)

No one is more averse than I am to "notions of "the Deity." And no one, I think, can be ignorant that the age of South was just the age in which the word 'knowing' was beginning to be confounded with that of forming notions. Nevertheless, there was a protest in the minds of South's contemporaries and of South himself against that confusion. If you will turn to the discourse which in most editions stands first in his Sermons, that 'On the Pleasantness of Religion,' you will, I think, agree with me. With the theology of that sermon Mr. Mansel is much more likely to agree than I am; as an exhibition of clear, powerful, racy English, every one must delight in it. But what I think will surprise you most is, that in what may be called in one sense a Utilitarian discourse, this is put forth as one of the charms and rewards of Religion, that it sets before us objects of thought which are infinite, and in which therefore we may roam for ever without satiety. Such is especially, according to him, the pleasure of religion, so far as speculation is concerned. Is Mr. Mansel willing to accept *these* words of South as a testimony in favour of his doctrine?

In the twenty-ninth Note to Lecture VII., there occurs this extract from CUDWORTH :—

"As it is certain that prescience does not destroy
" the liberty of man's will, or impose any necessity
" upon it, men's actions being not therefore future,
" because they are foreknown, but therefore fore-
" known, because future; and were a thing never so
" contingent, yet upon supposition that it will be
" done, it must needs have been future from all

"eternity: so is it extreme arrogance for men, be-
"cause themselves can naturally foreknow nothing
"but by some causes antecedent, as an eclipse of the
"sun or moon, therefore to presume to measure the
"knowledge of God Almighty according to the same
"scantling, and to deny him the prescience of hu-
"man actions, not considering that, as his nature is
"incomprehensible, so his knowledge may be well
"looked upon by us as such too; that which is past
"our finding out, and too wonderful for us."—(*Bampton Lectures,* pp. 404, 405.)

This passage would probably be quoted by many who desire to convict Cudworth of being a Platonist, as obscure. I make no complaint of it on that ground or on any other. It affirms that the knowledge which God takes of us is not measured by the knowledge which we take of Him, that the Infinite is not measured by the Finite, God's thoughts by our thoughts; all which I steadfastly believe. Whether Cudworth would have agreed with Mr. Mansel in thinking that the Infinite and Eternal are not subjects of man's thought, because they cannot be comprehended by his thoughts, those readers who are best acquainted with his writings may determine for themselves.

I need hardly have made this appeal to other readers, for the very next writer to whom Mr. Mansel appeals in his 'Examination,' BISHOP BROWNE, is

called in (Lecture III., Note 10) to confute Cudworth upon this very point. The author of the 'Intellectual System' had said, "Though we cannot fully
" comprehend the Deity, nor exhaust the infiniteness
" of its perfections, yet may we have an idea or con-
" ception of a Being absolutely perfect, . . . as we
" may approach near to a mountain, and touch it
" with our hands, though we cannot encompass it all
" around and enclasp it within our arms." Bishop Browne sets aside this distinction between Apprehension and Comprehension. He says, "If God is to
" be apprehended at all by any direct and immediate
" idea, He must be apprehended as infinite, and in
" that very act of the mind He would be compre-
" hended, and there is no medium between appre-
" hending an infinite Being directly and analogically." Bishop Browne, therefore, and Cudworth must pair off together; they cannot both form part of "the
" goodly array of Divines and Philosophers."

BERKELEY is mentioned in the Note to the Examination. There is a reference in the twenty-fifth Note of the fourth Lecture to the eleventh section of the seventh Dialogue of the 'Minute Philosopher.' In that Dialogue, you will perhaps remember, Alciphron meets all the arguments which Euphranor has urged on behalf of Christianity in their previous conversations with one clenching objection. "A
" thing demonstrably and palpably false is not to be

G

" admitted on any testimony whatever, which, at best,
" can never amount to demonstration.... You are
" not to wonder if the same sort of tradition and
" moral proof which governs our assent with respect
" to facts in civil or natural history, is not admitted
" as a sufficient voucher for metaphysical absurdities
" and absolute impossibilities. Things obscure and
" unaccountable in human affairs or the operation
" of nature may yet be possible, and, if well attested,
" may be assented unto; but religious faith can be
" evidently shown to be in its own nature impracti-
" cable, impossible, and absurd." When he proceeds
to explain this position, he maintains that every word
ought by its very nature to have some idea corresponding to it; that the words which are held most
sacred in the New Testament have no such idea corresponding to them. *Grace* is chosen as an instance.
For artists and ordinary men it has a signification; it
answers to comeliness or beauty. But that sense of
it which connects it with a Divine operation is altogether foreign to this. Theologians are continually
disputing about its meaning. *Euphranor* answers the
general objection by denying that there is an idea
which can be set out in the terms of a proposition
answering to every word which is in familiar use,
and which all men feel to have a most practical signification. The special instance is met by another.
What abstract idea can you fix upon as corresponding
to the word *Force?* If you assign one, may not an-

other philosopher assign another? Yet is not Force most real? Do you not attribute the greatest effects to it? He goes on:—" That which we admit with
" regard to Force, upon what pretence can we deny
" concerning Grace? If there are queries, disputes,
" perplexities, diversity of notions and opinions about
" the one, so there are about the other also; if we
" can form no precise, definite idea of the one, so
" neither can we of the other. Ought we not there-
" fore, by parity of reason, to conclude, that there
" may be divers true and useful propositions con-
" cerning the one as well as the other? and that
" grace may be an object of our faith, and influence
" our life and actions, as a principle destructive of
" evil habits and productive of good ones, although
" we cannot attain a distinct idea of it, separated or
" abstracted from God the author, from man the
" subject, and from piety and virtue the effects of
" it?" Then follows the eleventh section, to which Mr. Mansel refers. I extract all that can concern our subject.

" Shall we not admit the same method of arguing,
" the same rules of logic, reason, and good sense, to
" obtain in things spiritual and things corporeal, in
" faith and science, and shall we not use the same
" candour, and make the same allowances, in examin-
" ing the revelations of God and the inventions of
" men? For aught I see, that philosopher cannot be
" free from bias and prejudice, or be said to weigh

"things in an equal balance, who shall maintain the
"doctrine of force and reject that of grace, who shall
"admit the abstract idea of a triangle, and at the
"same time ridicule the holy Trinity. But, however
"partial or prejudiced other minute philosophers
"might be, you have laid down for a maxim, that the
"same logic which obtains in other matters must be
"admitted in religion. *Lys.* I think, Alciphron, it
"would be more prudent to abide by the way of wit
"and humour, than thus to try religion by the dry
"test of reason and logic. *Alc.* Fear not: by all the
"rules of right reason it is absolutely impossible that
"any mystery, and least of all the Trinity, should
"really be the object of man's faith. *Euph.* I do
"not wonder you thought so, as long as you main-
"tained that no man could assent to a proposition,
"without perceiving or framing in his mind distinct
"ideas marked by the terms of it. But although
"terms are signs, yet having granted that those signs
"may be significant, though they should not suggest
"ideas represented by them, provided they serve to
"regulate and influence our wills, passions, or con-
"duct, you have consequently granted, that the mind
"of man may assent to propositions containing such
"terms, when it is so directed or affected by them,
"notwithstanding it should not perceive distinct ideas
"marked by those terms. Whence it seems to follow,
"that a man may believe the doctrine of the Trinity,
"if he finds it revealed in Holy Scripture, that the

" Father, the Son, and the Holy Ghost, are God, and
" that there is but one God? Although he doth not
" frame in his mind any abstract or distinct ideas
" of Trinity, substance, or personality, provided that
" this doctrine of a creator, redeemer, and sanctifier,
" makes proper impressions on his mind, producing
" therein love, hope, gratitude, and obedience, and
" thereby becomes a lively, operative principle, influ-
" encing his life and actions, agreeably to that notion
" of saving faith which is required in a Christian.
" This I say, whether right or wrong, seems to follow
" from your own principles and concessions. But for
" further satisfaction it may not be amiss to inquire
" whether there be anything parallel to this Chris-
" tian faith in the minute philosophy. Suppose a fine
" gentleman or lady of fashion, who are too much
" employed to think for themselves, and are only
" free-thinkers at secondhand, have the advantage of
" being betimes initiated in the principles of your
" sect, by conversing with men of depth and genius,
" who have often declared it to be their opinion the
" world is governed either by fate or by chance, it
" matters not which; will you deny it possible for
" such persons to yield their assent to either of these
" propositions? *Alc.* I will not. *Euph.* And may
" not such their assent be properly called faith. *Alc.*
" It may. *Euph.* And yet it is possible those disciples
" of the minute philosophy may not dive so deep as
" to be able to frame any abstract, or precise, or any

"determinate idea whatsoever, either of fate or of
"chance. *Alc.* This too I grant. *Euph.* So that,
"according to you, this same gentleman or lady may
"be said to believe or have faith where they have not
"ideas. *Alc.* They may. *Euph.* And may not this
"faith or persuasion produce real effects, and show
"itself in the conduct and tenor of their lives, free-
"ing them from the fears of superstition, and giving
"them a true relish of the world, with a noble indo-
"lence or indifference about what comes after? *Alc.*
"It may. *Euph.* And may not Christians, with
"equal reason, be allowed to believe the divinity of
"our Saviour, or that in him God and man make
"one person, and be verily persuaded thereof, so far
"as for such faith or belief to become a real principle
"of life and conduct, inasmuch as by virtue of such
"persuasion they submit to His government, believe
"His doctrine, and practise His precepts, although
"they frame no abstract idea of the union between
"the Divine and human nature; nor may be able to
"clear up the notion of person to the contentment
"of a minute philosopher? To me it seems evident,
"that if none but those who had nicely examined,
"and could themselves explain, the principle of indi-
"viduation in man, or untie the knots and answer
"the objections which may be raised even about hu-
"man personal identity, would require of us to ex-
"plain the Divine mysteries, we should not be often
"called upon for a clear and distinct idea of person

" in relation to the Trinity, nor would the difficulties
" on that head be often objected to our faith."

I have quoted this unusually long passage partly because I was afraid of not seizing the point of evidence for which Mr. Mansel alluded to it, partly because it illustrates a difference which is of very great importance in this controversy. No persons would assent more readily to Berkeley's doctrine that the meaning of Grace as well as Force is to be tested by actual effects, and not by its correspondence with some abstract idea, than those who object most strongly to the doctrine of the Bampton Lectures, that there may be a regulative Revelation which produces effects upon the conduct though it is not the revelation of that which actually is. Berkeley's argument goes to show that that which in the truest sense *is*, which proves that it is by its operations, which the humblest person may therefore actually perceive and enter into, may be most inadequately represented by the notions and conceptions of our minds. When I contend for a human faculty which can ascend above the notions and conceptions of our minds and take hold of that which is, I contend for the very truth which Berkeley is asserting here. The interesting remarks which he makes in the latter part of the dialogue, about signs and the way in which they represent that which abstract terms cannot express, bring out this meaning, and throw, it seems to me, much light upon the Scriptural method of teaching. I say so with the less fear, because I am conscious that the great admiration which I feel for Berkeley as a man and as a thinker, does not hinder me from disliking the tone and style of many arguments in the 'Minute Philosopher.' It was impossible, even for a man benevolent and truth-loving as he was, to avoid the usual special-pleading and unfairnesses of an apology. I would make amends for what I said, perhaps harshly, of Mr. Mansel, that he appeared sometimes to be holding a brief for Christianity, by admitting that the charge applies to some of the best men of our own or of any country, and among others to him of whom a friend of another faith bore witness that he had "every virtue under Heaven."

The next reference is in the 2nd Note of the Third Lecture. It is to the 'Principia' of DESCARTES. (Part I, § 19.) "Thus then we shall never be fatigued with dis-"putations about the Infinite, for doubtless, since we "are finite, it would be absurd for us to determine any-"thing about it, and so to endeavour as it were to de-"fine and comprehend it." What can be more decisive in favour of Mr. Mansel's conclusion than this? Can the reader believe that only a few sections before the one in which this sentence occurs, these words are to be found? "I see not herein any difficulty for those "who have accustomed their minds to the contempla-"tion of the Divinity and who have had regard to His "infinite Prefections. For although we comprehend "them not, because the nature of the Infinite is

" such that our finite conceptions cannot comprehend
" it, we nevertheless conceive them more clearly and
" more distinctly than material things, seeing that
" being more simple and not being limited, that which
" we conceive of it is much less confused. Therefore
" there is no speculation which can help more to per-
" fect our understanding and which is more import-
" ant than this; since the consideration of an object
" which has no bounds to its perfections fills us with
" satisfaction and confidence." (§ 19.) I express no opinion about the method by which Descartes arrives at
this conclusion. It proceeds, you will remember, upon
those data which Locke's first book was written to
confute. Descartes supposes the idea of God to be
innate in man as well as the ideas of numbers and
figures. All I maintain is that the passage respecting the Infinite which Mr. Mansel has alleged, must
be interpreted, so far as our subject is concerned, by
the previous one, and that the author of it cannot
swell " the goodly array" of those who maintain the
doctrine of the Bampton Lectures.

I pass, not without sadness and reluctance, to the
next great name. It is that of PASCAL (Lecture IV.,
Note 19). It is not that I find anything in the
third article of the second part of the 'Pensées' which
is essentially different from that which I have just
quoted from Pascal's great countryman. The words
Mr. Mansel adduces are simply these:—" We know

"that there is an Infinite, and we know not its nature.
"So, for instance, we know that it is false that num-
"bers are finite; therefore it is true that there is an
"infinite in numbers. But we know not what it is.
"It is false that it is even; it is false that it is un-
"even, for by adding unity it does not change its
"nature. Nevertheless it is a number, and every
"number is even or uneven. It is true that that is
"to be understood of all finite numbers. It is quite
"possible then to know that there is a God without
"knowing what He is, *and you ought not to conclude
"that there is no God because we do not perfectly know
"His nature.*" 'Pensées,' Part II. Art 3. I might very
well rest upon the "parfaitement" in the last clause
(which clause, by the way, does not appear in Mr. Mansel's quotation) as a proof that Pascal was not contradicting anything I have said. I might remind you that
the whole of this passage is an argument with an atheist and apparently with a libertine too; that the writer
avowedly lowers himself to what he regards as his
opponent's point of view; and that nothing therefore
can be inferred from his statements as to his own
most inward convictions. I should like to say this
and to leave the subject. But I cannot honestly do
so. I am bound to admit that though this article
does not establish any direct sympathy between Pascal
and Mr. Mansel upon *this* point, it does contain what
seems to me the most frightful exaggeration of the
favourite argument about the chance of the Christian

being right, and the safety of his conclusion, which I believe is to be found in the writings of any good and wise man. There is a sort of satisfaction to one's English pride, in feeling that Butler, in a worse time, when he approached the edge of this argument, stopped so very far short of the point to which Pascal carried it. But this feeling is far outweighed by the pain with which one sees the exquisite subtlety which had been ripened in mathematical studies, as well as the real and deep earnestness of the believer, turned to such a low account; appealing to the evil instead of the good in the opponent; suspending a Gospel to mankind upon a calculation of chances. It is not right to suppress the fact that there exists in Christian literature such a parody as this upon Christian reasoning. "*Ce discours me transporte, me ravit,*" exclaims the atheist at the conclusion of it. I am afraid many of his class have felt the same transport in the reading of it, as they have drawn the conclusion that beneath Pascal's Jansenist faith there lay an unfathomable scepticism. Those who reverence and love his name, will rather believe that there was an infinite faith beneath this scepticism. They will turn to such passages as these as the warrant of that conviction. "Le Dieu d'Abra-
"ham et de Jacob, le Dieu des Chrétiens, est un Dieu
"d'amour et de consolation; c'est un Dieu qui rem-
"plit l'âme et le cœur qu'il possède; c'est un Dieu
"qui leur fait sentir intérieurement leur misère et sa
"miséricorde infinie, qui s'unit au fond de leur âme;

"qui la remplit d'humilité, de joie, de confiance, d'a-
"mour; qui les rend incapables d'autre fin que de
"lui-même. Le Dieu des Chrétiens est un Dieu qui
"fait sentir à l'âme qu'il est son unique bien; que
"tout son repos est en lui, et qu'elle n'aura de joie
"qu'à l'aimer; et qui lui fait en même temps abhor-
"rer les obstacles qui la retiennent et l'empêchent
"de l'aimer de toutes ses forces. L'amour-propre et
"la concupiscence qui l'arrêtent lui sont insuppor-
"tables. Ce Dieu lui fait sentir qu'elle a ce fonds
"d'amour-propre et que lui seul peut l'en guérir.
"Voilà ce que c'est que de connaître Dieu en Chré-
"tien."—(*Pensées*, Part II., Art 15, § 2.)

I am likewise referred in this note to BARTHOLO-
MESS. A passage from him occurs in Note 23 to Lecture III. "He who refuses to borrow some traits
"of resemblance from the moral part of creation,
"will be forced to derive them from the physical
"part of it, from the mathematical part, from the lo-
"gical part. He will make God in the image of the
"corporeal world, in the image of a geometrical or
"arithmetical magnitude, in the image of a dialecti-
"cal abstraction; continually in aiming at the Crea-
"tor he will be leaning on some spot or other of crea-
"tion." (*B. L.*, p. 344.) I do not know the work from
which this extract is taken, and I would not presume to
judge of the intention of the author. I should suppose, from the mere words as they stand, that he had

the same horror which I have of building up a notion of God from those forms of creation which most surely witness of Him; the same conviction that He must reveal Himself to us who are made in His image if He would not have us make Him in our image; the same conviction that the revelation must be a moral one in a perfect Man, and not through any physical or logical or mathematical part of creation. At all events, I could adopt his words as marking out conditions respecting our knowledge of God, which are as unlike as possible to those conditions by which the Bampton Lectures declare that we are bound.

JACOBI speaks next: "BEING without distinct "being ('ein Seyn ohne Selbstseyn') is altogether "and universally impossible. But an independent "being without conscious being, and again a con-"scious being without independent conscious being, "without substantiality, and at least an appended "personality, is quite as impossible. One as much as "the other is merely a clatter of words to which no "thoughts are attached. Then God is nothing, is "the not-being in the highest sense, if He is not a "Spirit. And He is no Spirit if the fundamental "property of a Spirit, self-consciousness, substanti-"ality, and personality are wanting to Him." (*Bampton Lectures*, p. 343.) Very high and noble doctrine it seems to me, true in every word and letter of it, confirmatory of the argument against Pantheism for which

I suppose Mr. Mansel originally quoted it; but as utterly inapplicable to the support of his doctrine respecting the knowledge of God as all that we have considered hitherto.

LEIBNITZ appears in the 12th Note to the Fifth Lecture, and again in the 10th Note to the Seventh Lecture. The quotation in the first note affirms that in other divine mysteries, as well as in those which he has been speaking of before, "reasonable minds will "always find an explanation which is sufficient for "faith, and *never* one which is sufficient for compre- "hension. We are told the *what*; but the *how* is be- "yond us and is not necessary to us." A Revelation of God in His Son is a revelation of the *what*, not of the *how*. I contend that it does tell us really what God is —not something else. The questions how or why, are not, it seems to me, involved in the debate at all. I never dreamed that the Nature of God ceased to be mysterious, ceased to be infinite, because I believed that the mystery had been made known, that the infinite had come nigh to us. Fully to expound the words of Leibnitz in this sentence, we ought to go into his whole doctrine concerning the reconciliation of Faith and Reason—the very subject of his Treatise; what I have said will be enough to show that on the ground of this passage alone Mr. Mansel cannot claim him as one of the goodly array.

The second allusion to him is only an allusion.

But it is to an earlier section of the Treatise, and Mr. Mansel has distinctly announced what he supposes Leibnitz to have maintained. These are his words:—" That the moral Providence of God cannot " be judged by the same standard as the actions of " men, see Leibnitz, Théodicée, De la Conformité, etc., " p. 32."—(*Bampton Lectures,* pp. 398, 399.)

No doubt Leibnitz does show, both by argument and instance, in *what* sense the Providence of God cannot be judged like the actions of men; whether in the sense of the Bampton Lecturer you shall judge. He is considering an objection of Bayle respecting the permission of evil. The ordinary rules of reason and justice cannot, argued the author of the ' Dictionary,' be applied to the actions of God by those who accept the Scriptural account of Adam and Eve. For what human tutor or parent would not be condemned by a human tribunal for exposing those of whose weakness he was aware to such a trial? Leibnitz replies to this reasoning by alleging that a human judge must avail himself of presumptions; that, no doubt, in a great majority of cases, those presumptions would be against the tutor or parent who should subject a child to such a risk; but that the case is conceivable of a person being proved by other evidence to be so good, so wise, so just in his ordinary proceedings, that this presumption would be quite overruled; that there *is* evidence of perfect wisdom, justice, and goodness in God; that therefore we have a right to call the presumption in this

instance on the other side invalid. He gives the result of this argument (§ 35) in these words:—" Ce n'est
" donc pas que nous n'ayons aucune notion de la
" Justice en général qui puisse aussi convenir à celle
" de Dieu; et ce n'est pas non plus que la justice de
" Dieu ait d'autres règles que la Justice commune
" d'hommes; mais c'est que le cas dont il s'agit est
" tout différent de ceux qui sont ordinaires parmi les
" hommes. Le Droit universel est le même pour
" Dieu et pour les hommes; mais le fait est tout dif-
" férent dans le cas dont il s'agit." He goes on to show (§ 38) that the appearances and probabilities which contradict faith may also contradict Reason; that one may as much demand that they should be set aside as the other. I trust you will consider the whole passage from the words "Une des choses," with which the section quoted by Mr. Mansel opens, to the end of § 38. I should be sorry that you or any reader should take my statement on trust.

Next appears STORR. A quotation from him is found in the 23rd Note to the Sixth Lecture. I will give it in the Latin, as I might misrepresent the author's purpose in a translation, and I do not think it is very important to the mere English reader.

" Cum enim longe aliud sit universe, rei *impossibi-*
" *litatem* intelligere, aliud *possibilitatem* rei *non* in-
" telligere; tum maxime in iis quæ tam vehementer
" ignoramus, sicut ea quæ sensui exposita non sunt,

" haud profecto impossibilia sunt continuo, quorum
" possibilitas, modus ac facultas a nobis non perspici-
" tur. Ergo, ut his utamur, philosophum non decet,
" universe negare divinam in condito mundo efficien-
" tiam, seu pro certo dicere, Deum ipsum (immediate)
" nihil quicquam conferre vel ad rerum naturalium
" consecutionem, veluti conservationem partis cujusque
" et speciei, quam genus animalium aut plantarum
" amplectitur, vel ad morales mutationes, ut animi
" humani emendationem, aut fieri omnino non posse,
" ut revelatio aliave eventa extraordinaria divinitus
" effecta fuerint."

I should not have supposed that a person who held this opinion would have been entirely at issue with me because I hold that *all* our knowledge may be traced ultimately to Revelation from God.

NEANDER appears in the following extract (Note 23 to Lecture II.) :—" Here, therefore, there occurred to
" him those reasons against a beginning of creation
" generally, which must ever suggest themselves to
" the reflecting mind, which cannot rest satisfied with
" simple faith in that which to itself is incomprehen-
" sible. Supposing that to create is agreeable to the
" divine essence, how is it conceivable that what is
" thus conformable to God's nature should at any
" time have been wanting? Why should not those
" attributes which belong to the very essence of the
" Deity, His almighty power and goodness, be always

" active? A transition from the state of not-creating
" to the act of creation is inconceivable without a
" change, which is incompatible with the being of
" God."*

I have thought much of this passage, have studied
it in its connection with the words of Origen, on which
it is a comment, and with the account of the theories
of Hermogenes and others which precedes it; and I
have been utterly unable to divine how it bears upon
any question which is at issue between Mr. Mansel
and me. I certainly never complained of the Bampton Lecturer for believing that the world was made
by the Word of God, and that the things which are
seen were not made out of things that do appear. I
should suppose, as Neander intimates, that such a faith
was the best deliverance from materialistic notions
of creation as well as from those notions into which
Origen fell in the desire to avoid them. I can admire
also, as much as Mr. Mansel, the historian's quick appreciation of intellectual difficulties upon this subject,
and the frankness and forbearance with which he sets
them forth. These excellencies, which are so characteristic of him, become still more conspicuous if we
follow out his remarks on Hermogenes, on the probable connection of his profession (that of an artist)
with the peculiar form of his doctrine; on the desire
which Origen showed to reconcile adherence to the
traditions of the Church with the exercises of his fancy

* " Church History,' English translation. vol. ii. p. 281."

on subjects which he supposed it had left open, etc. etc.; full of instruction, and quite as valuable for the method of treating such subjects which they suggest to theological inquirers, as for their own sake.

Two names yet remain on the list, besides those which I have omitted for the reason I have stated already; one I had nearly overlooked.

PROFESSOR LEE is referred to in Lecture V., Note 13 :—" It is plain," he remarks, " that, in any com-
" munication from an infinite Being to creatures of
" finite capacities, one of two things must happen.
" Either the former must raise the latter almost to
" His own level; or else He must suit the form of
" His communication to their powers of apprehension.
" . . . If we turn to Scripture, however, we shall see
" how this matter is decided. In God's dealings
" with men we find ' wrath,' ' jealousy,' ' repentance,'
" and other affections, ascribed to the Divine Being.
" He is described as ' sitting on a throne;' His
" ' eyes ' are said to ' behold the children of men;'
" not to mention other instances, which must sug-
" gest themselves to every one, in which God con-
" descends to convey to us, not the very reality in-
" deed, but something as near the reality as He sees
" it expedient for us to know."—(Professor Lee, *The Inspiration of Holy Scripture*, pp. 63, 64: 2nd edit.)

A very fair statement of the popular notions upon this subject. The word 'accommodation' seems to a number of persons to settle the whole question what these titles and names signify which connect the nature of God with the nature of man. To me it appears that the Scripture words, 'God made man in His own image,' 'The only-begotten Son is the express image of His Person,' are a solution of the difficulty, which no phrase or abstraction of ours ever can be. It is the inquiry which I have tried to raise in my Letters. I wish you earnestly to ponder it, and in the meantime to give every weight to the *ipse dixit* of Professor Lee to which you think it is entitled.

The last passage is taken from DROBISCH, 'Grundlehren der Religions-Philosophie' (Note 25 to Lecture IV.). The substance of it is gathered up in the last clause, "*Wir werden Gott nur durch Relationen* "*zu denken haben.*" I will not venture to affirm in what sense Drobisch may have taken this maxim. But I wish to say most emphatically that there is a sense in which I not only can accept it, but in which my whole book is the assertion of it. Indeed there is no point upon which I am so anxious that theological students should seek to understand themselves as on this; there is no truth which, I believe, may so much help to clear away misunderstanding between German and English students, and to make them helpers instead of hinderers of each other. The earnest and Christian Englishman is always, I suspect, disposed to think first of God as a Father. That name expresses to him a real relationship; it is no mere synonym of Creator; it connects itself with all that is most sacred in his home and human sympathies. The German almost as naturally grasps at an idea of God in Himself; and feels that he must perish if he loses it. Set up the Relation against the Absolute; glorify our own dear English faith, because it is ours; insult the German for what seems to us the vagueness of his aspiration; and we undermine our own ground. Fatherhood in God becomes *merely* at last a figure of speech formed after the likeness of our own earthly Fatherhood; an "accommodation" which it is well for us to preserve, because it produces certain good results in our minds, but which very soon our English honesty will reject, as it must reject whatever is merely invented for such an end. On the other hand, let the German scoff at our English indifference to ontology and our love for what is homely; let him wrap himself in his grand idea of an absolute Being; and soon he has no idea to wrap himself in; it passes into a mere conceit of his mind; the Being has vanished. But let us boldly say, 'Because we are really related to God, because 'we have a right, in the strictest, holiest sense of the 'word, to call Him our Father in the only-begotten 'Son, therefore we may ascend to the knowledge of 'Him as He is.' Let the Germans say, 'Because He 'absolutely is and we need to know Him, therefore 'does He speak to us through relations, therefore must 'we rise to Him through relations.' And then there will be no more cruel contentions between us. Each will refuse to part with that trust which has been committed to him. Each in fulfilling that will do justice to his neighbour. There will be a continual reciprocation of benefits. There will be a continual increase of Light to each from the other. I should care little about the fierce war which has been commenced in Oxford against the *Absolute* if I thought of it merely or chiefly as to the effect which it will produce on those who are seeking the Absolute. I dread it because it will teach Englishmen to regard the *relations* in which they stand to God as artificial and imaginary.

I can now bring this long Letter to a termination. With the exception of Hooker, to whom I referred in the last Letter, and of Butler, whom I must speak of hereafter, as he is the subject of a separate title in the 'Examination,'—and of two living prelates whose opinions I have no right or wish to canvass,—I have questioned each of the witnesses whom the learned Counsel on the other side has called to support his case. I entered upon the task because Mr. Mansel challenged me to it, and intimated that I had some good reason for declining it before. What is the issue? There remains of the goodly array of divines and philosophers enumerated in the note (possibly) Bishop Browne and Professor Lee.

I wish no reader to mistake the nature of this result. I have not proved in the least that Mr. Mansel's reading is not most extensive. I have the strongest conviction that he derived his quotations, not from indexes or at secondhand, but from a real study of the writers in which they occur. I do not believe that he designed to misrepresent them in any single instance. But the stronger our faith is in his learning and his wish to give his authorities faithfully, the more shall we be driven to the conviction that his mind is so wholly preoccupied and possessed by his opinion respecting the Eternal and Infinite, that he can hear nothing but echoes of that opinion whether he turns to the right or the left, to Fathers or Schoolmen, to English divines or to French or even German philosophers. His very respect for them compels him to understand them in that sense. An affectionate desire that they should not utter what seems to him dangerous nonsense, leads him to watch eagerly for words they may have dropped which look like an acknowledgment of the true philosophical faith, and makes him blind to any perverse exhibitions, even in closely neighbouring sentences, which might tempt him to suspect them of heretical pravity.

If I have been obliged to spend some time in removing the impression that the great men alluded to in the notes to the Lectures are supporters of the doctrines maintained in the text, I at least am thankful that I have been withdrawn for that time from personal controversy.

Very truly yours,
F. D. M.

LETTER VII.

SIR WILLIAM HAMILTON.

My dear Sir,

In the treatment of this controversy there is no topic of more importance than the relation between Sir William Hamilton, the Edinburgh philosopher, and his theological disciple in Oxford. It seemed to me when I read Mr. Mansel's Lectures and compared them with the Article on Cousin, in Sir William's Discussions, that there was scarcely an instance on record in which an eminent Philosopher had unwittingly done so much harm to a Divine, or in which the Divine had so thoroughly requited the injury by conveying a very unfair impression of the Philosopher. All the highest and most characteristic principles of Christian Theology, those that bear most upon the practice of life, were, it appeared to me, dwarfed and maimed that they might adapt themselves to the doctrine of the Unconditioned, which is set forth in the Review of Cousin. On the other hand, that most able Review, so full of instruction and interest to those who cannot assent to its negative conclusions, so rich in facts bearing upon the history of philosophy, and (especially in the notes which were added upon its republication in a volume) so precious to the theological student for its noble aspirations and its courageous inconsistencies, was forced to do duty as a mere weapon of attack upon a set of men whom it was desirable for the comfort of orthodox Christians to confute or to silence. And yet I could not help rejoicing that the experiment, however unjust to Christianity, however unjust to Sir W. Hamilton, had been made. For so I thought the weaknesses in his argument, which his knowledge, ability, and candour had been able to conceal, were brought to light; so it was shown that Man must pursue that Infinite and Eternal which his faculties cannot comprehend. And so also I trusted it would be proved that the Revelation of God will not submit to be treated as anything less than a Revelation of the Infinite and Eternal; that it cannot part with that which has made it dear to its friends, merely that it might gain a new engine against some of its foes. Divines have often appeared ready to purchase such engines at that price. If Mr. Mansel's was the ablest experiment of the kind, I hoped it might also be the last; its very ability might assist in demonstrating the falseness of the method upon which it proceeded, the unworthiness of the end at which it aimed.

Being very strongly possessed with these feelings,

I entered in my second Letter upon an examination of Sir W. Hamilton's Essay. At every step as I advanced, I felt a growing admiration for the honesty and the power that were displayed in it; at every step an increased conviction that the best antidote to anything that was wrong in it would be found in itself. I therefore extracted the statement—clear and beautiful as any I ever read—of the opinions that have been entertained respecting the Unconditioned as an object of knowledge or thought. I explained how much weight must attach to the judgment of a man with such great capacities for forming a judgment as Hamilton, respecting the impossibility of our conceiving the Inconceivable, or of our knowing that which we cannot conceive. I urged that his authority was seconded by all our own natural notions on this subject, that we were all inclined to vote a man a lunatic who supposed that " the greyhound could outstrip its own shadow, or " the eagle outsoar the atmosphere in which he floats, " and by which alone he can be supported" (*Discussions*, p. 14). All of us were ready to say with him, " How " indeed it could ever be doubted that the thought is " only of the conditioned may well be deemed a matter " of the profoundest admiration " (*Discussions, ibid.*).

Nevertheless I gathered from this same Essay that with a series of eminent men, " from Xenophanes to " Leibnitz, the Infinite, the Absolute, the Uncondi-" tioned, had formed the highest principle of specula-" tion." I gathered from the same Essay that Kant,

of whose speculations a most lucid account was given, had done his very utmost, in Sir William Hamilton's judgment, to get rid of such speculations, and yet that there " was contained in the bosom of his own philo-
" sophy " the germ of new efforts after the Absolute and the Unconditioned. The " theories," he said, " of " Fichte, of Schelling, of Hegel, and of sundry others, " are just so many endeavours of greater or less abi-
" lity to fix the Absolute as a positive in knowledge." I went on, still not departing from the Lectures, to speak of the progress of this same study in France, which was so unlike Germany in its philosophical character,—of the multitudes who crowded to Cousin's lectures in Paris.

Then I observed further that this pursuit of the Absolute, which it was " a matter of the profoundest " admiration that any should have engaged in," had also spread into our practical England, so that it was necessary to deliver lectures against it in the University Church of Oxford. The facts, all of which, except the last, I derived from Sir W. Hamilton's Essay, who had recorded them as if he deemed them of importance, I could not regard as insignificant. It was surely worth while to know how that which was a matter of profound admiration had come to pass. England being an extreme case, and also the one in which we were the most interested, I tried to discover how it was that we had been drawn into such inquiries; how those who boast of being emphatically experimental philosophers, could ever have ventured into that region which is apparently so opposed to experiment; how those who had been bred in the admiration of the Bible could approach the verge of that Rationalism which appears to make light of the Bible. I hinted, that perhaps our very pursuit of experimental science had led us to feel that we could not be tied and bound by the conditions of our own minds, that we must rise above them in order to see things as they are in the natural world. I hinted that our very study of the Bible might have led us to think, that there was a way to the apprehension of that which " eye hath not seen, nor ear heard, and it " hath not entered into the heart of man to conceive."

With some surprise I have read the following comment upon these statements in Mr. Mansel's 'Examination :'—

" Mr. Maurice's next discovery is equally sagacious.
" He has found out that the truth of a system of
" Philosophy may be ascertained by counting the
" number of its supporters at any given time, or even
" of those who attend to hear the lectures of a popu-
" lar exponent of it. He tells us, with an air of
" triumph, how the Philosophy of the Absolute has
" spread and flourished among disciples and listeners
" in Germany, in France, and finally in England;
" and he accounts for its progress in the last of these
" countries by the fact that it is 'the very effort which
" ' Bacon taught the student that he must make if

"'he would advance one step in the knowledge of
"'Nature.' Hegel would have been somewhat asto-
"nished to find himself described as the disciple of
"Bacon: Bacon would have been somewhat asto-
"nished to find himself described as the teacher of
"Hegel. Mr. Maurice however finds in the 'ear-
"'nest attention of Englishmen to physical studies'
"a proof of their sympathy with the metaphysics
"of Germany, and an explanation of the influence
"of German Philosophy on the Anglo-Saxon mind.
"He prudently omits to tell us that it has been taken
"up in England, so far as it has been taken up, as
"is not unusual with German speculations, at the
"very time when it has been generally abandoned in
"its own country. He prudently omits also to tell
"us that the method of Hegel is utterly opposed to
"that of Schelling, and that of Cousin to both of
"them; so that the followers of each diminish rather
"than increase the strength of the others, as regards
"the point of most importance—the means of attain-
"ing the proposed end. Both these facts somewhat
"militate against Mr. Maurice's arithmetical method
"of settling controversies in philosophy. But really
"such an argument is not worth a serious answer. It
"acquires a seeming plausibility in Mr. Maurice's
"hands, only from its connection with a third notable
"discovery, with which it may safely be left to stand
"or fall.

"Mr. Maurice's third discovery, for there are no

"less than three in this one Letter, is that Sir William Hamilton and the Bampton Lecturer both regard all who differ from them as fools or madmen. I was not aware before that this consequence followed from the mere assertion that they have pursued an erroneous method. Sir W. Hamilton can hardly have reversed the method of his predecessors more completely than Bacon did; and Bacon modestly compares himself to a cripple in the right way, who can outstrip a racer in the wrong. Sir W. Hamilton speaks of his antagonist M. Cousin, as a philosopher for whose genius and character he has the warmest admiration; and I am not aware of anything in the Bampton Lectures incompatible with a similar appreciation of most of the philosophers from whom the author finds it his duty to differ."
—(*Examination*, pp. 19, 20.)

I will merely observe upon this passage, which I am anxious should lose none of the effect which it can derive from the liveliness and wit of the critic;— 1st. That if I was so ignorant as not to know that Hegel and Schelling were not friends but opponents, Sir W. Hamilton probably was aware of that fact. It is he who has joined together their names, because they were both seeking, as he expresses it, to make the Absolute positive in knowledge. I joined them together as he did, and for the same reason. 2nd. That in what I said of Bacon I assumed him to be as unlike as possible to Hegel, just as I assumed those who had a reverence for Scripture to be as unlike as possible those who set Scripture aside. 3rd. That to consider the question, how the study of a particular subject by the most eminent thinkers for two thousand years was compatible with that subject being totally unfitted for human investigation, would not in general be described as an "arithmetical me-"thod of settling controversies in philosophy." 4th. That assuming Sir William Hamilton's data, it is not he, but I, that should pronounce the study of the Absolute to be *Lunacy*. I stated expressly, that the common sense of mankind would be in favour of that judgment.

And this is the explanation which I have to offer of another observation on which Mr. Mansel has commented in the following words :—

"In his second Letter, Mr. Maurice gives further "proof of his talent for making notable discoveries "in theology and philosophy. In the first Letter, he "found out that the Bampton Lecturer's method of "treating those from whom he differed was 'loud "'laughter:' in the present, he ascertains, with equal "sagacity, that Sir William Hamilton's method is "'ridicule' and 'jokes.' 'The kind of ridicule,' he "tells us, 'which Sir William Hamilton has poured "'upon such inquiries, was poured upon them in "'every age. Schelling knew such jokes from his "'boyhood; Hegel must have learnt them from "'doctors and jesters old and new.' The adversaries

"as well as the disciples of Sir William Hamilton
"have hitherto, by some strange delusion, taken him
"for a serious thinker; and his illustrious opponent,
"Cousin, in reference to this very article, speaks of
"him as 'the first critic of the age.' It was reserved
"for the genius of Mr. Maurice to make the brilliant
"discovery, that the Article on the Philosophy of
"the Unconditioned is an elaborate series of jokes;
"—a discovery the honour of which, it may safely be
"predicted, no rival critic will have the slightest
"wish to dispute with him."—(*Examination*, pp. 18, 19.)

Mr. Mansel has been good enough to extract the single passage of my Letter which could convey to any reader the impression that I regarded Sir William Hamilton's method as "ridicules" or "gibes," the single passage which could lead any one to suppose that I did not take him for a most serious as well as a most able thinker. I thank him for doing so. I am glad of the opportunity of saying that the word 'such' was an unhappy one. What I meant was this: There is contained in the article on the Unconditioned the *rationale* of ten thousand jokes which have been in circulation against transcendental philosophers from the days of Aristophanes to those of Mr. Mansel, and which were especially prevalent in the eighteenth century, when Schelling and Hegel were young men. Some of these jokes, I apprehend, were good ones, and profitable to those against whom they were directed; some very feeble and effete, which they could easily bear. To which class the jokes in the 'Examination' belong, I will not determine. I am far from affirming that they are 'such' as Sir William Hamilton would have approved or indorsed.*

But if Mr. Mansel has only been indulging a graceful humour in the former part of this article, he becomes very serious before the end of it. I call your attention, and the attention of every one of my readers, to the passage. The writer shall speak for himself; no account of his words could do them justice :—

"There is one other of Mr. Maurice's attacks upon "Sir W. Hamilton which it is important to notice,

---

* In Coleridge's 'Aids to Reflection' there is a very valuable passage, as it seems to me, on the distinction between *Mathesis*, or the process by which a student like Pythagoras arrived at a truth in Geometry, and the process of enunciating and demonstrating the same truth. More than twenty years ago—in some lectures now out of print—I urged that Sir William Hamilton's arguments against the studies of one of our Universities (the articles in the 'Edinburgh Review,' on that subject, were then comparatively recent) were based upon a neglect of this distinction. Mr. Mansel, of course, ignores it. But was it necessary to assume that *I* did not acknowledge it, and therefore to visit me with a storm of ridicule for treating Euclid as inductive and not deductive? (See *Examination*, p. 24.)

In the conclusion of this passage Mr. Mansel applies the same contempt to what I said of the Copernican doctrine, asserting that according to me, the believer in that doctrine must set aside the conditions of Relation, Difference, and Plurality. I am glad he has done so. The distinction to which I have referred is often overlooked in the case of Mathematics. But nearly all physical students confess its

I

"not so much for its own merits, as for the light
"which it throws on his method of controversy. Sir
"W. Hamilton, speaking with reference to the philo-
"sophy of the Unconditioned and the theology which
"its disciples have endeavoured to found upon it, ob-
"serves: 'True therefore are the declarations of a
"'pious philosophy :—'A God understood would be
"''no God at all ;'—'To think that God is as we can
"''think him to be, is blasphemy.'—The Divinity, in
"' a certain sense, is revealed; in a certain sense is
"''concealed : He is at once known and unknown.
"''But the last and highest consecration of all true
"''religion, must be an altar—'Αγνώστῳ Θεῷ—*To
"' *the unknown and unknowable God.*' On these words
"Mr. Maurice remarks, 'Now it cannot help strik-
"''ing any person brought up in our English reve-
"''rence for Scripture, that Sir W. Hamilton is here,
"''not by inference, but in direct terms, contradicting
"''St. Paul. *He* affirmed that the altar to the Un-
"''known God was *not* the last and highest consecra-

---

application of it to what we call the Experimental Sciences. They are perfectly aware that the conditions of Relation, Plurality, and difference, must be observed in stating and expounding the Copernican doctrine, but that those who used those conditions as chains to bind Nature and to direct their investigations into her secrets, were necessarily Ptolemaists. If he had lived in the sixteenth century, would not Mr. Mansel have been one of the ablest and most scornful of those logicians who put down the Italian opponent of the old doctrine when he went to Oxford in the company of Sir Philip Sidney to allege reasons against it ?

"'tion of true religion.—'*Him whom ye ignorantly*
"'*worship*,' he said, '*declare I unto you.*'

"Now it cannot help striking any person brought
"up in our English love of fair play, that Sir W. Ha-
"milton, by using the expression 'in a certain sense
"' revealed, in a certain sense concealed,' meant in
"direct terms to guard against this very charge of
"contradicting St. Paul, and to declare his conviction
"that the Revelation made by the Apostle was a very
"different thing from that proclaimed by the philo-
"sophy of the Absolute. I am not now inquiring
"whether Sir W. Hamilton was right or wrong in
"this conviction. It is sufficient that he had it, and
"that, having it, he employed language directly pro-
"testing against that very misinterpretation which
"Mr. Maurice has chosen to put upon his words.

"It is difficult to believe that Mr. Maurice did not
"know this; that he was not perfectly aware that Sir
"W. Hamilton is not 'in direct terms contradicting
"'St. Paul.' It is difficult to believe that Mr. Mau-
"rice did not use the language for the express pur-
"pose of creating in the minds of careless readers a
"prejudice against his adversary which he knew to
"be unjust. And it is right to draw attention to this,
"because Mr. Maurice, in the course of his work, is
"particularly severe on those writers who attempt to
"convict their opponents of error by the testimony of
"Scripture; 'turning,' as he expresses it, 'the bread
"'of life into stones for casting at your enemies.'

"And I call attention to it in this place, because the
"assault is not due to any previous provocation on
"the part of the victim. Mr. Maurice may perhaps
"think that the Bampton Lecturer has put himself
"out of the pale of fair controversy, and may be justly
"assailed by a method which is to be condemned in
"all other cases. But he has no excuse whatever for
"flinging the same missiles at the head of Sir W.
"Hamilton.

Mr. Maurice continues:—'I am not in the least
"'anxious to strain this point, or to use it as the
"'ground of a charge against Sir William Hamilton.
"'... God forbid that I should make a man an of-
"'fender for a word.' If so, we cannot help asking,
"why does he make a man an offender for a word?
"Surely, after solemnly calling upon God to forbid
"his making such a charge, he might have had the
"decency to erase from his page the sentence in which
"that very charge is made. But such a sacrifice was
"too much for Mr. Maurice's magnanimity. He pre-
"fers to fling the stone first, and then to say, 'God
"'forbid that I should throw it.'"—(*Examination*,
pp. 20-22.)

There are some omissions in the extract which is
the ground of this tremendous charge. I will supply them.

"I am not the least anxious to strain this point, or
"to use it as the ground of a charge against Sir Wil-
"liam Hamilton. *Every one knows what an excuse*

"*it would have been, if it had occurred in any Ger-*
"*man philosopher, for raising the cry that he wished*
"*to set aside Christianity as an obsolete and imper-*
"*fect religion, and to 'consecrate' a higher system.*
"But God forbid that I should make a man an of-
"fender for a word, *even if that word is the legiti-*
"*mate deduction from a proposition which is used for*
"*the purpose of making all other men offenders, and*
"*is vaunted as the basis of all orthodoxy! I rejoice*
"*to believe that Sir W. Hamilton meant to be a pious*
"*philosopher; I rejoice to discover in this very passage*
"*a wavering and uncertainty of mind, showing that*
"*the spirit within him demanded that resting-place in*
"*the Absolute and Eternal, which he said that men*
"*were not permitted, by the conditions of their intel-*
"*lect, to seek after.*"—(*What is Revelation?* p. 159.)

You will see that the words which Mr. Mansel left out contain the key to the whole meaning of this passage. For they prove (1) that so far from having an interest in convicting Sir William Hamilton of impiety, it was my object to show from this very sentence that he meant to be a pious philosopher, further evidence of which fact I went on to produce in a series of extracts from the other notes to the Review. (2) That I quoted that sentence from the Review because other sentences less strong and not illustrated and qualified by the context, had been quoted in the Bampton Lectures against different German and English writers for the purpose of showing that they set aside the teaching of the Bible. (3) That therefore, if I had designed to condemn Sir William Hamilton for a word, I should not only have belied all my own professions—I should not only have committed the atrocious wickedness which Mr. Mansel 'finds it difficult to believe' that I did not commit,—but I should have destroyed my own argument; I should have taken all the point out of observations which I believed had a point, and a sharp one, for the disciple, though none for the master.

As this is one of those awful charges against me of which I spoke in the beginning of these Letters—and as Mr. Mansel recurs to it afterwards as a support of the other, which he has endeavoured to make still more destructive of my character—I earnestly entreat those who have the strongest prejudice against me, the highest reverence for him, to examine into the proofs as they would into the proofs of any charge of forgery or of murder that are brought into an English court of justice. I ask them to consider whether I have misrepresented in any one point the process by which Mr. Mansel has arrived at his conclusion. I do not wish to add a word respecting the *animus* of the accuser as it is exhibited in the paragraph which follows. It is extracted from Archdeacon Hare's letter to the Dean of Chichester, and would no doubt be very apposite and very distressing if my design *had* been to make Sir William Hamilton an offender for a word. If all the evidence proves that that was not my design, the extract is as wide of the mark as any that is to be found in the English language. It may delight readers of very coarse minds, who are delighted with every *argumentum ad hominem*,—with whatever they think will inflict a certain amount of pain. It cannot produce the effect which Mr. Mansel "has difficulty to believe" that I was not aiming at, of misleading the most 'careless' reader,—seeing that the accident of my using the phrase " God forbid," which, like most others, is innocent or guilty according to the purpose to which it is applied, is what gives the quotation even a faint appearance of relevancy. If Mr. Mansel intended to revive an old controversy, or to mingle personal bitterness with a question of infinite importance, he may have succeeded. I know no other end he has achieved.

But as he has mentioned (quite incidentally) that Archdeacon Hare was an antagonist of Sir William Hamilton, I will take leave to say that nothing, I believe, would have delighted him more than to read in my Letter passages which would have convinced him that there was a heart agreement between him and one from whom in opinion he differed very widely. I know that he always sought for such agreements, and welcomed them if he found them in those who had denounced him in no measured words. And I know that my Letter respecting Sir W. Hamilton has led some who had previously disliked him to regard him as an earnest, noble ' hunter after truth.' That I wished them to receive this impression you at least will believe. And I trust that some Scotch friends and disciples of Hamilton who have complained of me for identifying his doctrines with the theological polemics which have been grounded upon them, will henceforth acquit me of any such injustice, and will join with me in thankfulness that Mr. Mansel's 'Examination,' if it has answered no other purpose, has at least made the difference between the objects, the methods, and the disposition of himself and of his assumed guide, strikingly manifest.

Very truly yours,
F. D. M.

P.S. The following note is appended to the quotation from Archdeacon Hare:—

"One moreover who did not hesitate to character-
"ize as 'belonging to the reptile order of litera-
"ture,' the work of one of the leaders of those *vulgar
"rationalists* whom Mr. Maurice (p. 250) regards as
"divinely appointed antidotes to check the extrava-
"gancies of mysticism. This, by the way, is another
"specimen of Mr. Maurice's fairness of quotation.
"In the Bampton Lectures (pp. 39, 40) I had
"spoken of the 'vulgar rationalism, which regards
"'the reason of man, in its ordinary and normal ope-
"'ration, as the supreme criterion of religious truth;'
"in contrast to the 'rationalism which agrees with
"'mysticism, in referring the knowledge of divine

"'things to an extraordinary and abnormal process
"'of intuition or thought.' The meaning of *vulgar
"rationalism* in this context is tolerably obvious, and
"affords no handle for an imputation. Mr. Maurice
"accordingly finds it convenient to alter vulgar ra-
"'tionalism' into 'vulgar rationalists,' and to print
"the words in italics apart from the context, to call
"special attention to their enormity. The two expres-
"sions are about as fair equivalents to each other
"as 'the vulgar tongue' is to 'a vulgar speaker.'"—
(*Examination*, p. 23, Note.)

Here again Mr. Mansel suspects his opponent of the blankest stupidity in order that he may convict him of base injustice. If I had meant to denote any of the rationalists, of the 'reptile' class, by the term vulgar rationalists, I should have stultified my own argument for the express purpose of contradicting the opinions of a friend to whom, as Mr. Mansel says, I am under unspeakable obligations, and whose judgment on any matter connected with German theological literature I should esteem above any man's. I took 'vulgar' just in the sense in which Mr. Mansel says he took it. The Italics might or might not be necessary; but they did not show that I had distorted the author's statements merely to confound my own.

LETTER VIII.

BUTLER.

My dear Sir,

When I was talking with you on the subject of Mr. Mansel's book and my answer to it, I found that you were at issue with me respecting the high opinion I expressed of Butler's Analogy. You could see a great worth in the Sermons upon Human Nature; but you could not overcome the feeling that the other and more popular book was a piece of ingenious special pleading, intended, like Mr. Mansel's, to show students what they must not investigate, rather than to guide their investigations.

The author of the Bampton Lectures is entitled to the full benefit of these complaints. They prove that his idea of Butler is at least a very prevalent one, not only among those who agree in his positions, but among those who entirely dissent from them. They give him a manifest advantage in contending with those who, like me, acknowledge that the Analogy has been one of their great teachers, and who yet have little liking for Apologies generally, and a special dislike for the class of Apologies to which you are inclined to refer Butler's. I felt, when I undertook my reply to Mr. Mansel, that the weight of opinion upon this subject—of opinion which I esteem highly —was against me. I was quite aware how many passages from the Analogy, that opinion could allege in its support. I enumerated, out of my own knowledge, a number of thinkers, each starting from a different point of view, who began their study of Butler with hope, and ended with disappointment. I had myself passed through enough of their different experiences to be able to sympathize, to a very great extent, with their irritation and despondency.

Nevertheless, I could not but testify of blessings which I could trace distinctly to this source. I was sure that I had learnt from Butler, (1) that the facts which surrounded us, and the facts of our own lives, are full of the deepest meaning, and are to be reverently examined for the sake of discovering that meaning; (2) that there is that analogy between the Constitution and Course of Nature and (what he calls) the Truths of Natural and Revealed Religion, which his title indicates, and that the more humbly we trace that Analogy, availing ourselves of all lights which Butler did not possess, or of which, from any cause, he could not freely avail himself, the more we should be rewarded. That the facts about us showed us this truth among others, that we are in the midst of a scheme with which we are very imperfectly acquainted, I could not doubt for a moment. That this truth might at times eclipse all others in Butler's mind, and might lead him to say, 'Do not look there or 'there; you will see nothing,' was very natural; and that the more he met with hasty and arrogant pretensions to knowledge, or with hasty and arrogant denials grounded upon the imaginary possession of knowledge, the more he would be tempted to press the proofs of the incomprehensibility of the Universe, and even of some of its commonest events, was also to be expected. But that he dreaded indolence far more than vigorous investigation;—that what he objected to most, in those very pretenders and deniers, was their impatience of steadfast inquiry, their easy acquiescence in a fashionable scepticism;—that he longed to make them think, and think earnestly, on those very subjects which are supposed by some of his modern disciples to lie beyond the bounds of al thought;—that his whole method stimulated and enforced this thought, however much some of his accidental words might seem to discourage it;—that even when he argued with men, something in the strain to which we have seen Pascal condescending, respecting the safety of one course and the danger of another, he intended the safety of thought and the danger of being without thought,—this I have been more convinced the more I have studied him, and have used one part of his writings to illustrate and expound another.

What Butler would have desired most, it seems to me, is, that wherever his book was used, wherever especially it was made a manual, these characteristics of it should be fully brought forth; if they were not brought forth, if any accidents of his arguments were prominently exposed and these thrown into the shade, his end would be defeated, his book would mislead. If, for instance, a teacher of Butler determinately adhered to the phrase *natural and revealed Religion*, he might be asked to define these words before he proceeded to his inquiry; one and another account of revealed Religion, as well as of Natural, might be rejected by his own fellow-disciples, and the objector might say, that till they had settled their differences, the Course and Constitution of Nature could prove but little. If, on the other hand, this teacher, being confessedly a believer in Scripture, consented to accept the Scripture substitute for that phrase;—if he was willing to speak of a Revelation of God, through Nature and through a divine Man,—he might be able to show that there was a strict analogy between those Revelations, and that the last, which was the highest, helped to the interpretation of the lower. The student would say to himself, Does the Revelation of the character, purposes, wisdom of God, in the person of Jesus Christ, contradict the previous Revelation of Him in the visible Universe? Are not contradictions which rested on the first taken away by the second?

The question whether Butler was to be treated in

this way or in directly the opposite way—whether his book was to show how men might find excuses for the Divine Government, or how God Himself vindicates it—might be a matter of comparative indifference in a Scotch University, or even in Cambridge, where, though he may be respected, he has not a greater influence than many others. But in Oxford, he has a special authority which has survived through many changes of feeling, and has been maintained by various schools. In the present day it seems to me more than ever important that the students there should know whether his name and method are used to crush doubts or to give a hope that these may be satisfied.

Much of what I said in my Letter will be intelligible chiefly to men who have passed through Oxford or are passing through it now. To some of them I am certain that it will be intelligible. I am sure they will know that the difficulties I have described are actual and pressing difficulties; that they do hinder the study of Butler, and do turn readers of him into infidels. To their earnest attention I commend the article on Butler in Mr. Mansel's 'Examination,' pp. 24–36. They will find in it (1) a series of extracts from Butler which correspond to certain passages in the Bampton Lectures. (2) A quotation from a passage in my book, wherein I point out how a student of the anomalies in the Moral world, or a student of the facts of the Natural world, may profit by Butler's method in arriving at an apprehension of the unspeakable worth of the higher Revelation which is made to man in the Son of God. (3) An allusion to a remark I made on the necessity for a real reconciliation of divine and physical methods inasmuch as a Museum was rising up to attest the serious devotion of Oxford to the study of Nature. (4) A quotation from a work of William Law in defence of Behmen's Theosophy.

(1.) The parallel passages in Butler's works and in the Lectures prove, what we all knew before, that Mr. Mansel had sympathized with those conclusions of the Bishop which refer to our incapacity of comprehending the Divine plans, and that he had skilfully blended this conclusion with the doctrine respecting the Unconditioned, which he had learned from Sir W. Hamilton. But (I speak to you who have a grudge against Butler, and would be rather pleased to convict him of an agreement with his modern disciple) consider whether the comparison which Mr. Mansel has forced upon us does not make most evident the actual difference between their methods, and between the ends at which they have aimed.

Take the different chapters in the first part of the Analogy. Observe that the first, " *Of a Future Life,*" instead of showing that it is impossible to know anything about that which is to be, argues for the extreme reasonableness of assuming Continuance, unless you have positive proofs of Dissolution. Observe that the second, on "*The Government of God by Rewards and Punishments,*" in like manner is designed to show, not the uncertainty of any inferences we can draw respecting that government here or anywhere, but the strong proofs that we have of its Uniformity, and the strong presumption that it will be the same in principle hereafter as it is now. Look at the third chapter, on "*The Moral Government of God.*" See how he argues, against all apparent contradictions, that the order of things here is in favour of Virtue and against Vice, and how he throws in the length of ages and the immensity of the Universe, not to make these inferences more doubtful, but to afford a hope that anomalies which we see may be in a process of removal. The fourth chapter, "*On a State of Trial,*" is equally based on the idea of a Uniformity in all the Divine proceedings. We are in a State of Trial as to our mundane interests. Is it not most reasonable that we should be in a state of trial as to our higher moral condition? Should there not be evidence to establish the contrary hypothesis if it were the true one? Read these sentences from the chapter which follows, "*On a State of Moral Discipline,*" and consider what they indicate respecting the object of the writer throughout his book. " Our being placed in a state of moral discipline "throughout this life for another world, is a Providential dispensation of things exactly of the same "kind as our being placed in a state of discipline

"during childhood for mature age. Our condition
"in both cases is uniform and of a piece, and com-
"prehended under one and the same general law of
"Nature." (*Analogy*, ch. v. art. 3.) The chapter on
"*The Opinion of Necessity as Influencing Practice*,"
is surely written for the very purpose of showing that
the positive evidence of an Order or Constitution, to
which human beings are subjected, and of their own
moral Nature, is not overthrown or shaken by any
theory that their actions are determined by some ir-
resistible fate. To all these chapters the one on
"*The Government of God, a scheme incomprehensi-
"ble*," succeeds. Had that chapter taken precedence
of all the rest;—had there been nothing previously
about a future state, a Government of God, an Education of Men by God;—had no evidence been produced to show that we are in the midst of an Order,
not of a Chaos,—the moral effect of the Analogy
might have been the same as that of the Bampton
Lectures. But seeing that it comes to wind up the
argument, and show that while we can know the
righteous purposes of God, there is a *Wisdom* devi-
sing plans for the fulfilment of those purposes which
we cannot penetrate, I conceive no two books in our
language have a more directly opposite tendency,
since one is occupied in the patient study of facts,
all leading to a positive result, and the other with
the learned and elaborate confutation of theories;
that confutation ending in a purely negative result.

K

(2.) Mr. Mansel is perfectly aware that the statement in p. 186 of my Letters did not profess to contain "the substance of Butler's teaching," but the results to which the use of his method might lead a person born in a different age from his age, and surrounded by different circumstances. He does not differ with me in holding that Butler's thoughts are germinant thoughts, which may bear fruits for other times such as they could not bear in his own; otherwise he could not suppose that they might be applied to the confutation of Hegel and of German Rationalism.

You may think that his deductions are more faithful than mine; some of his admirers may agree with me; some may say that Butler would have disclaimed us both. But I certainly should not be so unfair to Mr. Mansel as to say that he was pretending to give the substance of Butler's teaching in his second, third, or fourth Lectures, when he was manifestly assuming only to give us the results and applications of that teaching which had presented themselves to a very ingenious disciple, acquainted with a large amount of other literature.

(3.) If it were merely proposed that the studies of geology, chemistry, natural philosophy generally, should be added to the Oxford Curriculum—that such books as Sir Charles Lyell's, Professor Daniell's, or Humboldt's, should be made manuals on subjects of examination as well as books of Latin and Greek literature, or of Logic and Moral Science,—I quite agree with Mr. Mansel that there is nothing in the doctrines of his book which could in the least interfere with such a project. The establishment of a Museum pointed, I thought, in a different direction. It signified that Oxford was not merely encouraging her sons to read works on Physical Science, to learn what had been said or was already accepted upon any branch of study, but to investigate physical facts for the sake of arriving at discoveries. If I am mistaken on this point, I wish to be corrected. I hope it will be announced that the objects for which a Museum is founded in Oxford are not those for which it is founded in any other place. But, if I am *not* mistaken,—if the building signifies there what it signifies everywhere else,—then I apprehend it is of importance that the Oxford student should understand in what sense there is said to be an analogy between the studies in which he will be engaged in the Museum and those in which he will be engaged when he is in the moral or theological class-room. If he is told in the latter that the scheme of the moral Universe is imperfectly comprehended, and is told also that every fact in that moral Universe deserves to be studied and examined because it is under the guidance of a Being of absolute and eternal Goodness and Truth, who has revealed that Goodness and Truth to His creatures that through ages upon ages they may explore them and enter into them and dwell in them,—everything he meets with in that natural world which the Museum opens to him will be in strict analogy with this teaching; he will find himself there amidst wonders which baffle and confound him; he will find himself there, in spite of many discouragements and relapses, advancing step by step into light. But if in one, and in that which he has been used to regard as the principal department of his studies, he is told *only* of obstacles which cannot be surmounted; if there he is hemmed in with logical notions and conditions; if "thus far shalt thou go and no further" is written all around the walls of his lecture-room,— and the "no further" is interpreted to mean whatever belongs to the infinite and eternal Nature of God;—then I say he will either conclude that the same terms and formulas are hemming him in when he passes into the region of physical inquiries, and so all his efforts at the discovery of truths and the rectification of old errors will be abortive; or else he will feel that all is free and hopeful in one region, all barren and prohibitory in the other; he will inevitably prefer Physics to Morals, Nature to God. These consequences are too serious for one who regards the well-being of Oxford and of England with the feelings of a son, to be suppressed merely because they may be treated with utter contempt by the most popular doctor in the University. The indifference which such a man shows to the subject, his inability to comprehend even the nature of the fears with which many besides me are possessed, must add greatly to those fears.

(4.) If Mr. Mansel thinks that Behmen is a philosopher who would especially have welcomed the kind of inquiries into Physics which are carried on in a Museum—if he holds him to be a cautious, tentative, Baconian student, such as I have maintained that Butler is, and such as I desire that his Oxford disciples should be,—the panegyric of him and of his method by William Law, which he has quoted, is peculiarly appropriate to my case. If that is *not* the character which he ascribes to the Görlitz shoemaker, I am at a loss to know how so singularly inapposite an extract found its way into the 'Examination.' In despair of any other solution of the puzzle, I have been driven to suppose that Mr. Mansel had seen in some column of advertisements the notice of a volume of William Law's which I once undertook to edit. If he had opened the book, he would have discovered that it had nothing whatever to do with Behmen, that it did not even belong to the cycle of Law's mystical writings any more than the 'Letters on the Bangorian Controversy,' or the ' Serious Call ;' that it was simply an answer to Mandeville's ' Fable of the Bees.' Mr. Mansel knows quite as well as I do that into whatever perversions of thought or of language Law may have fallen when he was trying to represent the speculations of a man who wrote in German, which he did not understand, there were very few men, even in his own age, who possessed a greater command of pure and idiomatic English. However superior Butler may have been to him in other respects, he was, it will be generally admitted, immeasurably inferior to him in that. Supposing, then, that Mr. Mansel intended to confound me, either as a Mystic or as an unintelligible scribbler, a better *argumentum ad hominem* might have been chosen. Indeed I should have been slow to attribute that vulgarest kind of argument to a distinguished man, if he had not shown, in his extract from the 'Letter to the Dean of Chichester,' that he could stoop to it, and could even take pains to make his arrow venomous when he failed to give it a point.

Very truly yours,
F. D. M.

LETTER IX.

RATIONALISM AND DOGMATISM.—THE TWO METHODS OF ASCERTAINING THE FORCE OF WORDS.—APPEALS TO THE CONSCIENCE, ARE THEY DELUSIVE?—THE VALUE OF QUOTATIONS.

My dear Sir,

The pages 36–49 in Mr. Mansel's 'Examination' contain an exposure of my method of reasoning (of course he would not dignify it with that name), illustrations of it from passages out of various books of mine, denunciations of it by Dr. Candlish, Mr. Rigg, and others; together with a vindication of the Lecturer's own method, which I have, as usual, misrepresented, either from stupidity or malignity, or both. Unpromising as this statement is, I do hope that much may be learnt from these pages respecting the general controversy; that its nature and importance will become more evident from the remarks which I shall make upon them; that those remarks will allay instead of aggravating the personal irritation which there may be in the minds of Mr. Mansel and of his friends or mine. I encourage that expectation, because the more readers are aware that the question is one about two *methods* which concern all morals, all Theology, all the practice of life, the more seriously they will apply their thought to the subject, the less they will trouble themselves about me, or even about the distinguished persons who have written against me. At the same time they will see how inevitably, from the very nature of the case—(from the very vice, as Mr. Mansel would say, of my method)—I personally have been brought into the discussion; how impossible it has been for my opponents not to identify me with the cause I have been pleading; how easily and without any unkind prejudice they may have concluded that I must have a very spiteful feeling towards individuals, and be cloaking it under a pretence of tolerance and charity. As I said before, I am far from denying that my own clumsiness and moral defects, which are worse than any intellectual clumsiness, may have contributed to produce this impression. I cannot therefore hope entirely to remove it from the minds of those who have once entertained it, but, at least, it may cease to be an obstacle to any student in his own search after truth.

I will not repeat what I said in my second Letter on the word *Self;* on the way in which I have been led to connect it with actual personal experience; on the difficulty I have found in reducing it under a formal logical definition; but will ask you to bear those remarks in your mind when you read the following passage. I have ventured to supply from the

Letter of mine, whereon it is a comment, two sentences which Mr. Mansel has omitted, but which I think you will consider necessary for the full apprehension of my meaning if not of his.

"The first of these Lectures having commenced " with some remarks on Dogmatism and Rationalism, " Mr. Maurice commences his reply by giving his " own explanation of these two terms." Mr. Mansel proceeds, " After quoting the text *Cast first the beam* " *out of thine own eye,* he continues."—Of course the reader will assume that I quoted that text *at* the Bampton Lecturer. The whole passage stands thus :—

" In the eloquent peroration to his eighth Lecture " (p. 266), Mr. Mansel announces the oracle, *Know* " *thyself*, as the one guide to all safe thought upon " any subject. In cases like this, that oracle has " taken even a more distinct and awful form, as it has " issued from a more sacred shrine. ' *Cast first,*' it " has been said, ' *the beam out of thine own eye; then* " ' *shalt thou see clearly to take the mote out of thy* " ' *brother's eye.*' This principle, being so exactly in " accordance with the maxim of the Lectures, must, " we are bound to assume, have been diligently " weighed by the Lecturer. Before he proceeded to " charge any one else with Dogmatism or Rational- " ism, he went through, we may be sure, a laborious " process of inquiry, to ascertain what seeds of them " there might be in himself. But his performance "of that task, and his success in it, cannot absolve us from a similar one. I, at least, who have been warned by Mr. Mansel in some of the notes to which I have referred, that I have caught the infection of one or both diseases from greater men, am bound to look diligently for the signs of them in the only region in which I may truly judge of their nature or their effects."—(*What is Revelation?* pp. 194, 195.)

"The inuendo intended by this refined irony is tolerably obvious; but it is curious to observe the manner in which Mr. Maurice supports his implied accusation. The Bampton Lecturer had explained in his text and notes the meaning which he attached to the terms Dogmatism and Rationalism, by reference to their actual use at certain periods in the history of Philosophy; especially as applied in Germany to the followers of Wolf and Kant respectively. But this method of proceeding is not sufficiently philosophical for Mr. Maurice. Accordingly he forswears history and its applications, and retires within himself, to evolve the ideas of a Dogmatist and a Rationalist from the depths of his own consciousness. The portraits produced by this process may have more or less merit in other respects; but at all events they are utterly unlike any that appear in the Bampton Lectures. *There*, Dogmatism and Rationalism denoted certain methods of defence or attack, common to philosophy

"and theology. In Mr. Maurice's sketch, they de-
"note certain states of temper in which the defence
"or attack is made.* The one may be ascertained
"by the examination of a man's writings, and is
"therefore a legitimate object of criticism. The
"other can be ascertained only by an inspection of
"his heart, and the knowledge of it is therefore con-
"fined to the individual himself and to Him to whom
"all hearts are open. I do not deny Mr. Maurice's
"right to use his own terms in his own sense; but I
"do most decidedly deny his right to identify his
"terms so used with those of a writer who has dis-

* "Mr. Maurice distinguishes between a good and an evil Dog-
"matism and Rationalism; and his distinction, as regards the former,
"is curious enough. He says (p. 197), 'Every man knows that he
"'is a Dogmatist in the offensive, immoral sense, whensoever he
"'confounds that which *seems to him* or to any man with that which
"'*is;* that he is a Dogmatist in an honest and true sense, whenso-
"'ever he swears with deliberate purpose that something is, and
"'that from that no man and devil shall tear him away.' I am not
"interested in disputing Mr. Maurice's judgment of the 'offensive,
"'immoral Dogmatist;' as it is not in that sense that I have used the
"term; but surely his ingenious distinction is somewhat difficult of
"application. We are told that we are not to confound that which
"seems to us with that which is; but is there not a previous ques-
"tion, How came it to seem to us? If I honestly believe, after such
"investigation as I am able to give, that a certain doctrine is part
"of God's revelation to man, does it cease to be God's truth by be-
"coming an article of my belief? Or if whatever I believe is mere
"seeming, because it is my belief, what use can I make of the mere
"conviction that *something is,* if I am never to know *what* that
"something is, and am only warned against confounding it with
"anything that I think it to be?"

"tinctly stated that he employs them in another
"meaning. To call any man a Dogmatist or a
"Rationalist in the sense of the Bampton Lectures,
"is simply to say that his works contain reasonings
"of a certain kind: to call him by either of these
"names in Mr. Maurice's sense, is to assert that
"those reasonings were the result of a certain state
"of temper and feeling. The one statement may be
"borne out by direct citations from the works them-
"selves: the other is at best but a vague conjecture,
"and one which, whether true or false, does not affect
"the value of the reasonings themselves. Yet it is
"on a confusion of these two that Mr. Maurice's
"inuendo is based; and the whole of his edifying
"discourse on the mote and the beam derives its sole
"point from this ambiguity."—(*Examination*, pp. 36
–38.)

1. You will not be surprised—I was not—that Mr. Mansel should suspect "inuendo" and "irony" (the epithet 'refined' shows that he will not suffer me to monopolize that form of speech) in these extracts. Yet I do not see how I could have expressed my meaning otherwise. Though I objected to the negative use of the precept *Know thyself*, as excluding the knowledge of the Infinite,—the use which is made of it in the "Essay on Man"—I was sure there was a positive use of it which may indeed be said to descend from Heaven. I desired to show what I conceived to be the application of the oracle in this particular case. I

did not the least wish to deny that Mr. Mansel had so applied it previously. But I did think that unless each of us was willing to bring the words Rationalism and Dogmatism to the test of his own experience; —unless he was ready to ask himself, 'What kind of 'Rationalism, what kind of Dogmatism, does my con- 'science condemn me for using, what does it justify 'me in using?'—the discussion would lead to no satisfactory result, the condemnation of others upon either charge would be almost inevitably unjust.

2. Mr. Mansel pronounces that the "portraits pro- "duced by this process are utterly unlike any that "appear in the Bampton Lectures." Certainly; they professed to be unlike. I demurred to the process on which Mr. Mansel produced his portraits. I suggested another. They are open to comparison. I showed no desire to confound them.

3. The difference between these processes is said to be that one denoted certain methods of defence or attack common to Philosophy and Theology; the other, "cer- "tain states of temper in which the attack or defence "is made." Surely Mr. Mansel is not doing himself justice in this report of his own statement. He did not mean to *define* Rationalism as a mode of attack, because Rationalists have attacked certain propositions or principles, or Dogmatism a mode of defence, because Dogmatists have defended certain propositions. How has so accurate a writer fallen into this carelessness? Is it not because he has thought so much of the ap-

plication to particular writers of theology of that which he allows to be a general distinction, that the distinction itself has become identical with its accidental use? Certainly *I* did not denote by Rationalism or Dogmatism, states of temper in which merely an attack or defence is made. I thought a Rationalist might exhibit himself in looking at a picture, a Dogmatist in pronouncing on the binding of a book or the colour of a chameleon. But I do not think I am singular in treating them as habits or states of mind, rather than as modes of attack and defence.

4. It is said that "the one" (that is Mr. Mansel's sense of the words) " may be ascertained by the ex-"amination of a man's writings, and is therefore a "legitimate object of criticism." To this position I demur. I quite admit that if you begin with definitions of Rationalism or Dogmatism, you may contrive to bring a man's writings or certain passages in his writings under those definitions; and that you may then proceed to call him a Rationalist or a Dogmatist. But I deny that anything is 'ascertained' by this process, or that such criticism is of any value. You make and execute the laws by which you try the offender; they are generally *ex post facto* laws.

5. I " forswear history and its applications, to re-"tire within myself to evolve the ideas of a Dogma-"tist and a Rationalist from the depths of my own "consciousness." My sense of the words " can only " be ascertained by an inspection of my heart, and

" the knowledge of it is therefore confined to the in-
" dividual himself, and to Him to whom all hearts are
" open." These remarks, and the note, which is a
striking commentary upon them, raise anew the question which I raised in the tenth Letter of my book,
whether the disciple of Butler—the teacher of Butler
in Oxford—admits, in any sense, Butler's doctrine of
a conscience as applicable to practical life, or whether
he regards it as merely a theory in a book. Remember, the subject we are occupied with is not absolute
truth or falsehood. It is, according to Mr. Mansel's
own hypothesis, about " States of Temper." If conscience has no verdict to pronounce on *these*, on what
can it pronounce? What exercise has that supreme
faculty, that great lawgiver, of which Butler speaks?
Is it not a delusion? I would entreat any one carefully to read over the Sermons on Human Nature,
and the note to p. 37 of the 'Examination,' and ask
whether there is not more than an apparent—a radical and essential—opposition between them?

But let us try the general principle in the particular
instance. Mr. Mansel thinks that if I talk about my
experience of what is right or wrong in Rationalism
or Dogmatism, I am forswearing history, and setting
forth that which is individual and isolated. If it is
so, of course what I say goes for nothing. Every one
would exclaim at once, ' I never felt anything like
' that. Your description does not reveal anything to
' me that I ever did right or wrong, any judgment that

'I ever was forced to pass on myself. What is it to
'me? How can I know the meaning of words better
'for it?' This will of course be the answer, if I have
taken a piece out of a private chapter of my own
story, to which there is nothing answering in the story
of mankind. It was just because I was sure that this
was not the case, that my words *would be* responded
to by numbers, that my experience was not a peculiar one, but the vulgarest, the most universal of all,
that I dared to set it down. And because I am convinced that all our deepest experiences,—all our experiences of the struggle between right and wrong, between
the apparent good and the real good,—are common
experiences which the peasant and the scholar share
together,—it is therefore that I do not think Butler
was uttering vain and idle words when he put forth
his idea of Human Nature as inseparable from the
idea of a Conscience; though I hold, as I have said
before, that St. Paul's doctrine of a Flesh and a Spirit
is higher and more practical and more universal than
his, one which relieves it of its embarrassments, one
which connects it with the perception of the Eternal
Truth; and that St. John's words respecting the Light
that lighteth every man, show how the human has its
root in the divine, how the mystery of a conscience
is intertwined with the mystery of a Revelation.

(6.) Mr. Mansel goes on to say:—" As I did not
" use, and never intended to use, the terms Dogmatism
" and Rationalism in the sense which Mr. Maurice

"has affixed to them, I could hardly, as he recom-
" mends, have adopted his mode of determining their
" meaning, before mixing them with any theological
" associations. Nor was there any need to do so.
" Mr. Maurice has chosen to give to both terms a
" moral meaning, in which they are made to denote
" certain states of mind, which he himself describes
" as 'altogether detestable.' I have given them an
" historical meaning, in which they may certainly be
" connected with intellectual errors, but convey no
" moral imputation whatsoever. My object was not to
" exhibit the temper or personal character of any in-
" dividual or number of individuals; but to show how
" certain philosophical principles had in opposite ways
" affected, consciously or unconsciously, the theolo-
" gical teaching of certain writers. And to do this,
" it was necessary to have recourse to theological in-
" stances." (*Examination*, pp. 38, 39.)

I observed, you may remember, that a person looking at a picture or a natural landscape, and asking
himself continually, '*Why* are we to admire this?'
'*Why* is this beautiful?' would be, in my sense of
the word, an offending rationalist; just as a man who
merely brought to the study of the same picture or
natural landscape certain canons or notions about
beauty, which he had formed or inherited, and substituted them for an earnest contemplation of it, would
be an offending Dogmatist. And since the idea of
Rationalism and Dogmatism which I derive from this

L

example is not changed in the least when it is applied to the highest subjects of metaphysics and theology, I might plead with some plausibility that I am not confounding moral errors with intellectual, more than Mr. Mansel. But I do not avail myself of that plea. I believe it is an unsound one. I confess that I regard the question as a moral one, in its lowest forms as in its highest. I confess that I think the student of the picture who lets the 'why' or the canons come between himself and the object, is yielding to an immoral, I will repeat my former expression, to a 'detestable' habit. I find these habits in "my own consciousness;" they meet me everywhere in history. Each man, I believe, has to fight them in himself, in his children, in every person upon whom he has any influence. He can fight them just so far as he acknowledges that he himself and that each of them is called by God to a right exercise of his faculty of Reason, to a right reverence for the Judgments and Decrees of past ages, and that he himself and each of them has a conscience to which God is speaking, and which bears witness for the right and against the wrong.

7. But as I do not pretend that my method fixes the limits between intellectual and moral error,—as I do not see why it is necessary that we *should* fix these limits, if our only object, for ourselves and for others, is to check the tendencies and tempers which lead to either,—so I cannot admit that Mr. Mansel's charges

against individuals whom he has attacked, "convey no moral imputation whatever." It seems to me that he is yielding to a great delusion when he takes up this opinion, and that it accounts for the union of that courtesy of tone towards his opponents, for which his critics gave him, not too great, credit, with the want of substantial 'English justice' which I complained of. Standing entirely aloof from the Rationalists and the Dogmatists whom he was censuring; not feeling that their errors were his errors, not feeling that it behoved him to examine 'states of temper' at all, he could with the kindest intention and in the gentlest voice speak of men as holding a system which was less "logical then undisguised Atheism," less "religious than unmixed idolatry;" and when he was introducing individual names, could attribute direct or implicit denial of the 'revealed doctrine of the Atonement' to men who were bound by their subscriptions to hold it, by their ordination vows to preach it. So far as I am concerned, I should make no complaint of Mr. Mansel for fixing the last or even the first charge upon me. I should only ask that if he did fix it, he would call it by its right name, that he would frankly own it was a 'moral imputation,' just as much as the charge of wilful lying which he has in terms brought against me in his 'Examination.' There is no want of ordinary 'English justice' in that charge. The grounds of it are stated. I can meet them, and perhaps rebut them. It is the vagueness and uncertainty of charges which may mean something very criminal, or may be explained away to mean nothing criminal at all, which in the schools will *possibly* be understood as referring only to a particular mode of attack or defence, which will be at once treated in the world as marking out men for ecclesiastical censure and public disgrace,—it is this which in my own name and in the name of many more I solemnly protest against.

8. I was led in my Fourth Letter to complain of an outrage upon English justice and philosophical method, by Mr. Mansel's application of his remarks upon Rationalism and Dogmatism to those who attacked or defended the revealed doctrine of the Atonement. On reconsidering the passage regarding this subject which Mr. Mansel has extracted from my book, I find one sentence which I regret, and wish to retract. I "said, It was therefore *convenient* to leave the whole "subject in vagueness." This sentence did not imply to my mind, nor could it convey to the reader's, anything like the notion of 'a favourite expedient' for misrepresenting and injuring an opponent. It expressed, at most, the belief that just at that moment Mr. Mansel found vagueness more suitable to his purpose than direct statement would have been. But the phrase did convey *that* insinuation, and therefore is of the same *kind* with one which I considered unfair in my own case. I own at once that I had no right to use it. There is no merit in saying so, for I believe that by yielding to the temptation of imputing a

wrong motive to another, I weakened my cause. My business was to show how Mr. Mansel's method involved him unwittingly in an act of unfairness. By suggesting the thought that he had resorted to it for some convenience of his, I turned the point of the argument in a wrong direction; I made it less evident why the wrong with which I reproached him had been committed. But as to the substance of the charge, I retract nothing. I feel more strongly than I did before what the consequences of adhering to his method must be, how great the duty is of adhering to an opposite method. Let me state the case to you, availing myself as I proceed of all the increased knowledge which I have gained from Mr. Mansel's notes, of the objections which he and others feel to that opposite method of mine, of the indignation with which it inspires them.

9. The question, what is denoted by these words, "the revealed doctrine of the Atonement," is probably the one in our time which is most occupying the attention of English Episcopalians, of Scotch Presbyterians, of all the religious sects and schools into which England and Scotland are divided. Since lawyers like you require that a man should have some standing-ground, some personal interest, before he appears as a party in a cause, I may say that a number of journalists have again and again told the Bishops of our Church that they are culpably negligent in allowing me to remain one of its ministers while I

believe what these journalists suppose me to believe on this subject. Dr. Candlish, the most eminent of Free-Church Ministers, took the opportunity of a visit to England some six years ago, to explain how very differently I should have been treated if I had accepted his confession, and had been within the reach of his discipline. Men of the highest character, learning, and influence, who are alluded to in the note on Mr. Mansel's first Lecture, have been subjected to something little short of official censure, for opinions on this subject of a different kind from mine, but not more odious to the religious journals. Not many years ago a series of Sermons was preached in the church in which Mr. Mansel's Lectures were preached, some of them by Prelates of the Church, and was introduced to the world by a preface proceeding from the then Vice-Chancellor of the University. In that preface Dr. Magee's Lectures on the Atonement were distinctly announced as a standard of English orthodoxy. All later heresies were said to have been foreseen in that book; by it they might be judged and condemned. Now, widely as I may differ from some of the opinions of the excellent man who was understood to be chiefly pointed at in those sermons and in that preface, I have said before, and I say again, that I do not accept Dr. Magee's Lectures as a standard of orthodoxy, and that if either the University or the Bishops instead of or in addition to the subscription to the Prayer-book and the Articles, require a declaration that his doctrine is the revealed doctrine of the Atonement, they will compel me, and I believe multitudes besides me, not to quit the English Church,—that, thank God, they can never do,—but to renounce all share in its ministrations or its possible emoluments. It is better to say so openly and at once. I ask that no one may be hindered from holding Dr. Magee's opinions upon the Atonement, who feels that they are compatible with his faith in Scripture, in the Prayer-book, and the Articles; I cannot pretend that they are compatible with mine.

10. My reasons for objecting to Dr. Magee's statement, and to all less elaborate and learned statements of the same kind, I have given in the course of my Letters on Mr. Mansel's Lectures and elsewhere. I should not repeat them if they did not contain the interpretation of certain expressions in my book which have given particular offence to Mr. Mansel, and which, more than once in the 'Examination,' he has quoted against me. That all Nations, civilized even more than barbarians, have attached great worth to Sacrifices, Dr. Magee has, I apprehend, shown perhaps more satisfactorily and learnedly than his predecessors in the same path. That he has overstated the importance of that fact I do not believe. That he has been right in supposing that the intention of these sacrifices was to propitiate the gods to whom they were offered, and to avert the punishment of the sins of those by whom they were offered, no one, I think, can dispute. That

the needs which were expressed in these Sacrifices were actual human needs, and that the feelings and notions which accompanied those needs are likely to present themselves, in some form or other, in every age and country, I am fully convinced. That the great subject of the Gospel is a Sacrifice, and that the Sacrifice must bear a relation to all the needs expressed in the heathen sacrifices, I should proclaim everywhere. But I find these words written. *"All things are of God, who hath reconciled us to Himself by Jesus Christ, and hath given to us the Ministry of reconciliation. To wit, that God was in Christ reconciling the world unto Himself, not imputing their trespasses unto them, and hath committed to us the word of Reconciliation."* Because I receive this text as announcing St. Paul's idea of the Gospel which was entrusted to him, I must believe that that Gospel meets the needs expressed in the heathen sacrifices by *reversing* the notions which were embodied in them. Reconciliation with a righteous and living Being was what men wanted. But because these schemes of reconciliation *were all of men ;*—because they guessed the characters of their gods from themselves ;—because they necessarily imputed to them the low and selfish tempers which were in themselves,—therefore every plan of propitiation was an attempt to persuade the gods not to punish offences which, for the world's sake and for the offender's sake, ought to have been punished; which attempts became more base as the minds of the sin-ful petitioners became more base. When *all things* were declared *to be of* GOD, when He became Himself the Propitiator, the Reconciler, the Atoner,—the message of a Lamb who taketh away the sins of the world was exchanged for the message of an offering to remove the punishment of particular men; that message could be proclaimed to the conscience for its deliverance from the burden of sins; it might be proclaimed to all, without exception, because it was the news of an Atonement, of an actual Union of the Righteous God with man in the Son of God and the Son of Man; because it was the message of a Spirit given to men that they might be delivered from their own inward evil, and reformed in the image of the Father.

11. Now the danger I apprehend from Dr. Magee's statement of the doctrine of Atonement is nothing less than this, that it has given and does give a scholastical sanction to that which I hold to be the most perilous of all popular tendencies, that is to say, the tendency to reproduce the notions of Paganism in the forms of Christianity, and so to set aside the "*revealed* doctrine of the Atonement;" or, as I should express it, the Revelation of the Atonement of God with Man in Christ, which the Apostles preached, and which we are sent to preach.

When therefore the most scholastic and the most popular preacher in a University from which that dictum respecting Archbishop Magee so short a time before went forth,—himself proclaiming in one of his notes his deference to the same authority,—took for granted " a revealed doctrine of the Atonement," against which certain objections had been raised, or which had been defended by unlawful arguments, and when he set down certain persons as Rationalists for dissenting from this doctrine, was it very unnatural or unreasonable that a person holding the convictions I have expressed, should ask that the charge might be more definite? Was not the question too serious, pressing too strongly upon individual clergymen, upon the whole Church, upon each of our flocks, to admit a refined distinction about intellectual errors and moral evils? Am not I abetting moral evils if I mislead those who are trusted to me respecting the moral nature of God? Have I any other way of curing them of moral evil but by declaring how He has revealed Himself as the extirpator of it, as the deliverer of the sinner from it?

12. Such issues, such great moral issues, being, it seems to me, involved in this question, I have never hesitated to use very strong language in denouncing those Pagan notions which mingle, as I think, with our popular notions of the Atonement, with our popular Theology generally. But what do I mean by popular notions? I mean, as I have explained, those which I find in myself; "in the depths of my consciousness," as Mr. Mansel would say. I should rather say, *not* in the depths

of it, but on the surface of it. For when I look into the depths of it, I find another faith altogether different from this. I find that which answers to the cry, "*Lo, I come: in the Volume of the Book it is written of me, to do Thy will, O God;*" I find that which asks for a real Atonement and Reconciliation with God, and which embraces the message that there is One who has made it and in whom it stands firm for ever.

The signs of that deeper faith, of that response to the divine Revelation, I find however not only in myself but also in those popular divines against whose semi-Paganism I have often been disposed to exclaim. I find in them words which have stirred my inmost heart, and which I am sure have been kindled by a divine Inspirer. I find also in those same persons, when they are exposing the Romish doctrines of indulgences, of intercession, of an unfinished salvation, the boldest denunciations of that mixture of Paganism with the Gospel which I fancy I detect in them. Nay, Mr. Mansel informs me that Mr. Rigg, upon whose authority and judgment he places great reliance, accuses me, among other Anglican divines, of Paganism. So that I am not singular in my dread of this peril, or in my conviction that it requires to be continually watched against and denounced. But because I agree entirely with Mr. Rigg, and know possibly better even than he does that I have this Pagan tendency in me,—as I venture to think it is also in him,—I do not feel myself justified in selecting passages which would prove this person or that to have uttered sentiments respecting the Atonement which I regard as Pagan. I am rejoiced to believe that he would disclaim the imputation, feeling that it did not describe his real purpose. I am rejoiced to think that he could produce sentences of his which would show how unfair a representation of him had been deduced from the others.

13. This is Mr. Mansel's bitterest complaint against me. *He* produces extracts from books, which show that the writer is adopting the mode of attack or defence, which he describes by the name Rationalism or Dogmatism. *I* talk of popular opinions, current notions, sayings of divines, and never produce chapter or verse for any of my charges. My answer is, When I am finding fault with an individual man, I do take pains to produce chapter and verse. Whatever he may say of my Letters respecting him, they were not deficient in this respect. And if I were following his method,—if I began with laying down certain definitions of my own which referred to " intellectual errors," though they might at any moment dilate themselves into most inconvenient " moral imputations,"—I should be obliged to do as he does, to take passages from authors which would serve as illustrations of *my* notions about them—not, perhaps, at all of *their* meaning. But since my desire is to get all the help I can, and to give all the help I can,

in resisting evils which I feel to be threatening the life of each one of us, of our country, of the whole Church, and in sustaining the good which I believe God is keeping alive in each of us, in our land, in the whole Church, I will—God aiding me—incur all risks of offending the leaders of scholastical thought and popular feeling amongst us by pointing out what I hold to be the great religious and moral corruptions of the age, and will *not* run the risk of offending any simple Christian by fixing upon him, or upon some teacher whom he loves, as an example of those corruptions.* I will tell my countrymen, and tell myself, that we are men of like tempers and passions with the worshipers of Moloch and of Mammon and of Siva. I will tell them that there is no security against our falling into that worship in the fact of our being surrounded with a Christian atmosphere, in our

---

* Between the publication of the first and second editions of my 'Theological Essays' a number of comments upon them appeared in the religious journals, from which I might have extracted confirmations of all my most startling accusations against the popular theology, even while those accusations were vehemently disclaimed. (*E. g.* I was called a heretic by a religious journal for maintaining that the words, "Behold the Lamb of God, which taketh away the sin of the world," should be read as they stand, and that 'punishment' should not be substituted for 'sin.') But though the corporate character of these writings takes them out of my rule against assuming the isolated statements of individuals as evidences of their general opinions and faith,—though they represent faithfully enough the different parties of which they are organs, *as parties*—there is that in each party which they do not represent, and which justifies the best men of

having been brought up to acknowledge all the mysteries of the Christian faith. I will tell them that God Himself is our only deliverer from false and dark notions of Him, and that if we do not trust in Him to save us from them and to give us the true knowledge of Himself, they will creep in upon us, and overcome us, and mould all our orthodoxy into their likeness. And if A. B. and C. being in conspicuous places, from which they are influencing others, should seem to me to be abetting directly or indirectly this evil, I will do what in me lies to counteract their lessons. But if I have any occasion to speak against them, I will add that I do not hold them to be worse men than I am, and that I am satisfied they have a better and nobler spirit in them, which is confessing the true God and rendering probably a more acceptable homage to Him than I render. I will say this because I hold it to be true, and because I ought to say it; though I know perfectly well that such language will lead Mr. Mansel to suspect me of hypocrisy, and though it is sure to draw forth such pungent re-

each party in disclaiming them. On the whole I thought it safer and honester to let people condemn me for saying that there is that element in popular theology which earnest laymen complain of publicly, which clergymen confess privately in sorrow and shame, than to produce instances of it either from anonymous or known writers. I used the privilege of a second edition for another purpose, viz. to erase certain passages which had given unnecessary pain without asserting any important principle; passages which Mr. Mansel has sought out and preserved.—See 'Fraser's Magazine,' Nov.

marks as the one which he has quoted against me from Dr. Candlish:—" It would really seem as if the "author's notion of candour and charity were this: "blacken your opponent to the utmost pitch of black-"ness, by making his belief thoroughly odious, and "then generously whitewash him with the insinua-"tion that after all his belief is a sham." If this description is a true one, as I am sure Dr. Candlish and Mr. Mansel consider it to be, it cannot do me much harm; the inward insincerity and wickedness in the sight of God of such a character as Dr. Candlish has portrayed, must make all the appearances it may present to men of little moment. If it is not exactly a faithful portrait, I may still have much to answer for having led eminent men, through my violence or stupidity, to suppose that it is impossible to denounce with intense earnestness what one feels to be the mischievous acts and teachings of others, without exalting oneself or denying them to be capable of all excellence. I am certain that this cannot be impossible, otherwise there can be no reformation wrought in the earth; since the evils that prevail in an age have always hitherto been opposed by those who were bitterly conscious of those evils in themselves, and therefore sought to extirpate them. Mr. Mansel takes me to be a person who believes himself pure and other men foul; for these are the words with which he winds up the article:—

"It is doubtless easier and more sweeping to cen-

"sure classes than to cite individuals; but that Mr. "Maurice should have succeeded in persuading him- "self that the one course exhibits the very cream of "brotherly kindness, while the other is remarkable "only for 'hard and proud words spoken against "'those who were crying out for truth,' is one of "those extraordinary self-delusions which it is easier "to expose than to explain."—(*Examination*, pp. 48, 49.)

As I have shown you that I did not charge Mr. Mansel but myself with uttering "the hard and proud words;"—as I believe he cannot by any raking together of evidence from my books, even from those passages which I deliberately left out, prove that I have ever given myself credit for "the cream of brotherly kindness;"—as I have not declined to cite individuals that I might have the pleasure of censuring classes, but that I might not make either individuals or classes responsible for principles which I believed were injuring both,—I think that he has misunderstood me a little, and the method for which I have been contending altogether.

Very truly yours,
F. D. M.

LETTER X.

THE PURE REASON AND REVELATION.

My dear Sir,

The passage of Sir William Hamilton respecting Kant, which I quoted in my book on Revelation, and to which I have referred in one of these Letters, shows what importance he attached to the Critical Philosophy. It *might*, he thought, have led to the abandonment of all inquiries respecting the Absolute and Infinite; it had in fact been the starting-point for some of the most elaborate and resolute of those inquiries. Mr. Mansel recurs to the subject often in his Lectures. He speaks of Kant as one who made himself a transgressor by building up that which he had destroyed. In a note to his fourth Lecture he used this language:—

"If there is but one faculty of thought, that
"which Kant calls the Understanding, occupied with
"the finite only, there is an obvious end to be an-
"swered in making us aware of its limits, and warn-
"ing us that the boundaries of thought are not those
"of existence. But if, with Kant, we distinguish

" the Understanding from the Reason, and attribute
" to the latter the delusions necessarily arising from
" the idea of the unconditioned, we must believe in
" the existence of a special faculty of lies, created
" for the express purpose of deceiving those who
" trust to it."—(*Bampton Lectures*, p. 264.)

As this distinction of Kant's had always seemed to me of great practical importance for reasons of which I shall speak presently, I commented severely on the phrase " Faculty of Lies." It seemed to me one which was not respectful to a great man, and one which must confuse the judgment of the reader. Mr. Mansel replies to what I said by bringing several heavy charges against me. I am anxious that you should consider not only the matter of these charges, but the exact terms in which they are expressed.

" Mr. Maurice, as we have already seen, is fond
" of superlatives; whatever may be thought of his
" manner of applying them. We have seen what are
" his notions of 'philosophical method and English
" 'justice,' and of 'the most flagrant outrage' upon
" both. We have now to examine his specimen of
" 'language scarcely paralleled in controversy.' If
" I am not mistaken, the examination will tell a
" curious tale of Mr. Maurice's 'philosophy,' or
" 'justice,' or both. It will scarcely be believed by
" those who have read only Mr. Maurice's invective,
" that the whole of the above note, concerning a
" 'faculty of lies,' is taken from the direct assertion

" of Kant himself; that the charge of falsehood
" against the reason originates with the very phi-
" losopher whom Mr. Maurice so indignantly vindi-
" cates from the imputation of having 'believed in
" it;' and that it occurs, not in that portion of his
" writings in which he is attempting 'to overleap the
" ' bounds of his own philosophy,' but in that in which
" he is laying down those bounds with the utmost
" strictness. Mr. Maurice must be well aware,
" though many of his readers may not be, that one
" of the principal divisions of Kant's best-known
" work is entitled 'Transcendental Dialectic,' and
" treats of certain illusions which the author declares
" to be inherent in the constitution of reason itself.
" In the introduction to this division, the illusion is
" stated as follows:—' In our reason, subjectively
" ' considered as a faculty of human cognition, there
" ' exist fundamental rules and maxims of its exercise,
" ' which have completely the appearance of objective
" ' principles. Now from this cause it happens that
" ' the subjective necessity of a certain connection of
" ' our conceptions is regarded as an objective neces-
" ' sity of the determination of things in themselves.
" 'This illusion it is impossible to avoid.' And sub-
" sequently, in the second book of the same division,
" Kant says, 'Such arguments are, as regards their
" ' result, rather to be termed sophisms than syllo-
" ' gisms. . . . They are sophisms, not of men, but
" ' of pure reason herself, from which the wisest can-

"not free himself.' And again: 'The paralogism
"'has its foundation in the nature of human reason,
"'and is the parent of an unavoidable, though insolu-
"'ble, mental illusion.'"—(*Examination*, p.   .)

Then, after quoting a passage from a pamphlet of his own respecting Kant, which I have no doubt I ought to have read, and should have been much better for reading, but which I never have read, or, to the best of my remembrance, seen, he proceeds:—

" Mr. Maurice probably never saw the above pas-
" sage, of which the note in the 'Bampton Lectures'
" is merely a repetition. If he has seen it, his offence
" must assume a much graver character. But even
" without this assistance, it is difficult to imagine
" how a professed historian of philosophy and reader
" of Kant could have been so profoundly ignorant
" of one of the best-known parts of his best-known
" work, as to refer a criticism belonging to Kant's
" speculative philosophy, in which he fixes the limits
" of pure reason, to his practical philosophy, in which
" he attempts to overleap them. But accuracy of re-
" ference is not Mr. Maurice's *forte;* and it would
" be cruel to demand such drudgery from a man of
" his inventive and invective genius. He had found,
" or thought he had found, an interpretation which
" enabled him to bring a serious charge against his
" adversary: it was too much to expect that he should
" take pains to ascertain whether his interpretation
" was the right one. What is the exact resemblance

" between Butler's principle of conscience and Kant's
" pure reason, with its three ideas derived from the
" three forms of the logical syllogism, and the neces-
" sary illusions involved in each, is a question which
" must be left to be expounded by Mr. Maurice
" himself, who has already shown his talent for ma-
" king discoveries in Butler. If the above mistake
" was made in honest ignorance, it says little for
" Mr. Maurice's qualifications as an historian of phi-
" losophy: if it was made in wilfulness, or even in
" culpable negligence, it supplies an edifying com-
" ment on his own language a few pages back: 'Of
" ' all outrages upon philosophical method, and upon
" ' ordinary English justice, which are to be found in
" ' our literature, I believe this is the most flagrant.'"
—(*Examination*, p.   .)

Once more:—

" But Mr. Maurice is not merely the historian of
" philosophy and the *arbiter elegantiarum* of contro-
" versy: he is also himself a philosopher; and in that
" capacity he proceeds to show that the Kantian
" Reason, or something equivalent to it, is indis-
" pensable to the reception of religious truth. 'The
" ' question,' he says, 'is concerning that which *is*
" ' and that which is not; whether there is any
" ' faculty in man that can be brought to perceive
" ' that which is, and to reject that which is not, *in
" ' any matter whatsoever;* whether that faculty is
" ' extinguished when we are called upon to pay the

"　'highest reverence and worship to a certain object
"　'or objects; or whether it is this to which God
"　'himself appeals.' This faculty, he has just before
" told us, 'is not special, but human,' and 'is worth
"　'more than all the notions of the understanding,
"　'because it takes hold of that which is substan-
"　'tial.'

" Truly a wonderful faculty, and one of which
" Mr. Maurice has made some wonderful uses. But
" notwithstanding the magnificence of its promises,
" we need some surety for their performance. Mr.
" Maurice regards this faculty as the criterion of
" truth in the highest things, as that to which God
" himself appeals in His revelation to man. Mr.
" Maurice, then, believes in the Trinity on the wit-
" ness of this faculty, distinguishing that which is
" from that which is not. But his Unitarian neigh-
" bour, possessed of the same faculty (for it is not
" special, but human), and using it as honestly as
" Mr. Maurice himself, arrives at the conviction that
" the doctrine which Mr. Maurice accepts as one of
"　'the pillars of his own being and of the Universe,'
" is a contradiction and an impossibility. Who is to
" decide between these two conflicting exhibitions of
"　'that which is'? "—(*Examination*, p.　.)

There are several accusations here which I will take in order. Unimportant as they are to the reader so far as they only concern me, they suggest questions which may be of the greatest interest and value to him. Mr. Mansel accuses me (1) of pretending to be an historian of philosophy; (2) of complaining of a charge against Kant which his own words fully justify; (3) of absurdity in suspecting a relation between Butler's doctrine of the Conscience and Kant's doctrine of the Reason; (4) of absurdity in thinking that God appeals in His Revelation to this faculty of Reason. I begin with the first and least interesting of these subjects.

(1.) If I had professed to be an historian of philosophy, the sneer which has been bestowed upon my pretensions would have been not an "insulting" but a well-merited one. Those who have looked into the book which has exposed me to that sneer, will know that I have again and again disclaimed the dignity of an historian. Twenty-two years ago I was asked by an eminent man, not generally identified with Rationalists and Mystics—the late Rev. Hugh James Rose,—to write, in an Encyclopædia which he was editing, a sketch of the progress of Moral and Metaphysical enquiries. I entered with much fear upon a task which he thought I might perform without disgrace to a work to which eminent men had contributed and were contributing. In spite of very kind words which had been spoken to me about the article by men whose esteem much abler writers might prize, I felt, when I read it as a whole, that it was exceedingly crude and unsatisfactory. Being asked by the present proprietor of the Encyclopædia to prepare it for separate publication, I began, eleven years ago, to rewrite it. He has not generally seen cause to complain of the great "haste" in composition which Mr. Mansel imputes to me. He has rather thought that in my determination not to copy existing manuals, but to give such accounts as I could of each author I spoke of from my own reading, and often in his own words, I was drawing unfairly upon his own patience; he would say, perhaps, upon the patience of my readers, though the *vel duo vel nemo* included in that list may not be worthy of very serious consideration. Certainly, if I proposed to myself fame, or any more tangible reward, nothing can be more absurd than the pains I have bestowed on so meagre a sketch. I am quite aware that Oxford doctors will scorn it; I am quite aware that it will find no favour with Germans, or with our own Liberal schools. Nevertheless I have persevered, having a hope, supported by one or two unexpected encouragements, that hereafter, when the name of the writer is forgotten, it may assist a few students who are struggling with difficulties which I have struggled with; may show them that there is a connection between the thoughts of the schools and the life of the world; may give them hints for tracing better than I have traced the relation between the inquirers of one period and those of another; may cheer them with the thought that a divine Teacher has been with men of all ages, in the midst of their confusions, and that He will not desert their contemporaries or them. These egotistical remarks, however silly they may appear to Mr. Mansel, will be tolerated by you, and they may help you, I fancy, to understand better the next point which is at issue between him and me.

(2.) In writing the sketch to which I have alluded, I have felt it an especial duty to preserve, not in name only, but in fact, the chronology of human inquiries. I mean, that I have been afraid of imputing to earlier men the forms of thought which belong to the students of a later age; while ~~time~~ I have been also most anxious to show how the same doubts do present themselves in different forms, and demand a solution in the earliest times and in the latest. It seems to me that the German historians of Philosophy,—valuable as they are for their great diligence and erudition,—being cradled in Metaphysics,—knowing Kant and Hegel before they know, at least as philosophical students, Plato and Aristotle, or certainly Anselm and Aquinas, are apt to read the Greek and mediæval writers by the light which falls from their own schools, and to explain them by reference to those schools. An Englishman, it seems to me, may profit by the practical habits of his country—I had almost said, by his ignorance of and his inaptitude for Metaphysics—to escape this inversion. He may watch the men who transmit the torch more truly, may report the steps which they have run more faithfully, because he does not know so well who or what is coming next. I confess for myself that I have been desirous to reserve the exact study of German philosophy, as such, till I come to it in its own proper period, believing that the preparation of interest in the speculations of previous generations will give me—not the large acquaintance with the books that contain it which Mr. Mansel and others possess, but—such a perception of the different lines of thought which different men have followed, and of the points at which they join older lines of thought, as students tell me they miss in the works of some men of great acquired knowledge, and even of great metaphysical acuteness.

I was quite aware that this method of proceeding would put me at a great disadvantage in any conflict with a man who had armed himself for a battle with the German Schoolmen by a recent and diligent study of their writings. No one in England would have been less competent to appear as their champion than I should have been. But I had no such object. I was looking at the whole subject from an English point of view; the interests for which I was contending were English interests. When therefore I had to speak on such a subject as Kant and the Critical Philosophy, I did not begin with explaining any opinions which I might hold about him and that philosophy. I did not bring forth, out of my slender stores of reading, passages from Kant which Mr. Mansel might at once have overpowered with passages from his extensive reading; I took the statements which I found respecting him in Sir William Hamilton, confirmed and commented upon as they were by Mr. Mansel. Against these at least no objection could be raised; Mr. Mansel's learning and his arguments would not be employed to show that these were worth nothing. The objection to Kant was, that though anything but favourable to ontological speculations, he had unawares conceded the existence of a faculty which transcends the limits of experience, and busies itself with subjects which lie beyond the conditions of the understanding. This was the first charge. Connected with it was another, which is especially considered in Mr. Mansel's seventh Lecture, that he admits the existence of a faculty of Practical reason, which is concerned with the principles of universal morality. Any one entering upon an examination of the Critical Philosophy as such, is bound to mark most carefully this distinction between the speculative and the practical reason,—is bound to deal with all those passages in Kant's writings which attempt to fix the objects and the laws of either. I hope, whenever I come in the course of my sketch to the inquiries of the eighteenth century, I shall not spare any diligence that may be requisite for this purpose; though I shall certainly not be able to satisfy Mr. Mansel either about my methods or my results. But in this book these questions only were present to my mind. Is there or is there not a faculty in us which looks beyond appearances to the thing as it is in itself? Is or is not this the strictly human faculty as distinguished from the faculties which belong to different individuals? Is or is not this faculty that to which the revelation of God's own Nature and Being is addressed? Or is this to be called rather a "faculty of lies"?

Now I have no doubt that in the pamphlet of Mr. Mansel, which I have not seen, he carefully announces that he is criticizing one part of Kant's writings and not another; that he is occupied with the speculative and not with the practical Reason. There is nothing in the note to which I referred, so far as I see, which determines its application in the same manner. But if there were, the observation with which Mr. Mansel wishes to crush me is a pure sophism. No doubt Kant is investigating in the part of his work to which Mr. Mansel alludes, the laws of the Reason as such. But he assumes, as Mr. Mansel himself has told us, that that Reason overleaps the boundaries and conditions of the *Understanding*, and it was with this overleaping that I was concerned. I was speaking here of the speculative Reason so far as it is that which takes cognizance of Being as distinguished from appearances. I was not confounding it with the practical Reason, though I did hold, and I will show you hereafter why I held, that *we* may perceive a union between the practical and the speculative Reason, which Kant did not perceive. But, will you credit it? That very extract which Mr. Mansel has given from Kant's Transcendental Dialectic, to prove that accuracy of reference is not my forte, is a maimed quotation, one that breaks off in the middle of a sentence, the remainder of which, as I think you will admit, explains in what sense Kant holds that there are illusions in the pure Reason, and confounds the whole argument which Mr. Mansel raises upon the first part of the extract. After the words, "Eine Illusion, die gar nicht "zu vermeiden ist," he adds, "so wenig, als wir es "vermeiden können, dass uns das Meer in der Mitte "nicht höher scheine, wie an dem Ufer, weil wir jene "durch höhere Lichtstrahlen als diese sehen, oder, "noch mehr, so wenig selbst der Astronom verhindern "kann, dass ihm der Mond im Aufgange nicht grösser "scheine, ob er gleich durch diesen Schein nicht be- "trogen wird."*—(*Die Transcen. Dialek., Einleitung.*)

Now this illustration shows, I apprehend, clearly, that Kant believed the faculty of the Reason to be liable to a class of illusions of its own, precisely as he believed the senses to be liable to a class of delusions of their own. The illusions are altogether different;

---

* Translated thus by Meiklejohn: "This illusion it is impossible "to avoid, just as one cannot avoid perceiving that the sea appears "to be higher at a distance than it is near the shore, because we see "the former by means of higher rays than the latter; or, which is "a still stronger case, as even the astronomer cannot prevent himself "from seeing the moon larger at its rising than sometime afterwards, "although he is not deceived by the illusion."

the nature of each must be inferred from the nature of the faculty itself. And if these illusions warrant us in calling one faculty a faculty of lies, they warrant us in giving the same name to every other; they warrant us in saying that we are living in a lie. The professed object of Kant's Transcendental Logic is to guard against the illusions of the Reason, as he expresses it, " Den Schein transcendentaler Urtheile " aufzudecken und zugleich zu verhüten dass er nicht " betrüge;" just as there is a similar discipline to prevent the senses from deceiving us. There is, indeed, a method recommended in the extract which Mr. Mansel gives from his own pamphlet for avoiding the perplexity. Kant had only to say that there is no distinction between the Reason and the Understanding, and to call the illusions of the Reason the impotence of the Understanding; then the illusion would cease. The German, I suspect, had considered that way of cutting the knot as seriously as Mr. Mansel. It was the natural and obvious one which his inclination would have led him to embrace. It was the pressure of evidence, the sternness of his actual observation, which compelled him to refuse it. At all hazards, in spite of all apparent contradictions, he must confess that there is that in us which grasps at the Infinite and Eternal,—which will not be content with phenomena, or with any arguments and deductions from phenomena.

But though the analogy of the senses and their

illusions is amply sufficient to justify any one in not denying the existence of a pure Reason because it may be exposed to illusions, I am perfectly aware that there is a startling difference between the deceptions which occur to us while we are conversing with appearances, and while we are attempting to look beyond appearances. This difference has been felt most painfully by those who have accepted Kant's belief in a higher faculty. They have admired his honesty for not allowing any anomalies to hinder him from rejecting the evidence of facts; they have owned this to be the true test of a scientific inquirer. But they have also been certain that paralogisms and antinomies lying so near the root of their being,—belonging to their very nature,—must be very terrible, and must demand a more perfect solution than his Transcendental Logic, however valuable in itself, can supply. These persons have been driven to ask whether the impossibility of finding such a solution did not lie in the nature and limitations of the Critical Philosophy; whether there must not be something to complete the inquiry into the nature and demands of our faculties, viz. a full inquiry into the Objects of those Faculties. The visible world meets the senses and gives them their objects. What meets the faculty which rises above sense and experience, and gives it its object? Is not that "appearance of objective principles" in the Reason, which Kant speaks of, precisely the indication of this want? Could there be a more faithful exposition than that phrase contains of the need in the highest region of our being, of something to commune with it and save it from the endless and frightful contradiction into which it falls from making its own thoughts its objects?

Hence, I apprehend, arose the demand for that Philosophy of the Absolute and the Infinite in Germany which Mr. Mansel thinks may be got rid of by simply denying the existence of any faculty which transcends experience. Closely connected with that demand, though only in some cases *consciously* connected with it, arose the feeling in many religious Germans, that the Gospel or the Christian Church might fill up the void which Kant had discovered and left. I will not allude to the various movements, in one direction and another, Evangelical and Romanist, to which this thought has given the impulse. I do not say that the records of these movements are not of great worth for Englishmen; I do not say that there have not been movements in England which have corresponded to them. Still the question about these paralogisms and antinomies of the Reason, presents itself to us in quite a different form from that which it takes in Germany. It *does* present itself to us, though the names Paralogisms and Antinomies may sound as strange to us as any specimens of the Caffre dialect. We admit them in fact, though we have no words for them; they give rise to many murmurs; they lead to much indifference and despair; they are discoursed of under other titles in sermons; the preacher tries sometimes to turn them to account, sometimes to remove the prejudices against all divine lessons which the discovery of them awakens. And most devout Englishmen will, I think, be disposed to admit that there must be paralogisms and antinomies in any faculty which is created to seek after that which is above all sense and experience, and which does not perceive that that which it seeks is coming to meet it, is seeking for it. Stated in our own way, in our own conventional forms, this is one of our approved commonplaces. Hundreds of passages might be quoted from divines to whom Kant's name is a dream or a horror, which apply the story of the man who, when his eyes first began to be opened, saw men as trees walking, to the eye of the spirit when God first says Ephphatha to it, meaning that hereafter it should behold Him clearly. Translated into philosophical phraseology, what is this but the mistaking of the perceptions of the Reason for its object? You may easily persuade Englishmen to believe the faculty which they are told is spoken of in Kant's Critique on the Pure Reason a faculty of lies; but you will not persuade them, if they are serious, godly men, that what they speak of under the name of their inward eye is a faculty of lies; though they know all too well, and will confess with profound sorrow, how quickly, how of necessity, it falls into lying, when it is not in communion with its true Enlightener.

No doubt, it is difficult to connect these practical conclusions of our countrymen with those which Germans have arrived at by so different a process. But there are encouragements in attempting that course, and there are motives which, I believe, make it necessary at this time. The encouragement lies in the fact that almost fifty years ago, Mr. Coleridge, then a most unpopular writer, regarded by the public sometimes as a poetical, sometimes as a metaphysical madman, in circumstances eminently unpropitious, in a book which was published in a provincial town, made a still more startling application of the doctrines of the Critical Philosophy, and especially of the doctrine respecting the illusions of the pure Reason which is now under our consideration, to the political controversies of the day, and that his words, little as they might be understood or heeded at the time, wrought so secretly and so effectually upon the minds of his younger contemporaries, that there is perhaps no Conservative speech or pamphlet of our day which is not different from what it would have been if the Essays in the 'Friend' had not been written. In these Essays, you may remember, he treats the attempts to found a Constitution on the idea of the Rights of Man, as originating in those assumptions of the pure Reason which Kant has pointed out in his Transcendental Dialectic. The course of thought which he pursues in the 'Friend' may have struck many as unintelligible and absurd. Nevertheless it enabled some to reconcile the experimental wisdom for which Burke contends in his Reflections, with deep moral convictions respecting human rights which they could not part with. It enabled them to do justice to the changeable without losing their faith in the permanent. I am bound in gratitude to record that opinion, because the younger men of our day, whether they call themselves Liberals or Conservatives, do not know what they owe to Coleridge. Deeming that some of us have spoken extravagantly of him, they are half-disposed to adopt again the cant of the vulgar wits who tried to persuade us and our elders that he was an impostor. There are too many eminent men of letters who are ready, from different antipathies, to favour that reaction—too many grave and reverend signors, who once were glad to profit by Coleridge's arguments, and even to take part in building his sepulchre, but now suspect that the arguments may not always support their conclusions, and that the sepulchre may be a reproach both to their fathers and to them—not to make it a duty that those who still feel unspeakable obligations to him, should take every suitable opportunity of confessing them.

(3.) But even if there were no encouragement from past experience, a wish to save some of the truths which English thinkers have vindicated from neglect and denial, a still stronger desire to make those fruits available for our English *people*, would stir me to the effort of maintaining that there is that faculty of which Kant bore witness. We have seen in the last letter how Mr. Mansel treats that belief in a Conscience which was the strongest of all beliefs in the mind of his master. Whenever I speak of that faculty as being available for any practical purposes, whenever I assume that there is that in me which passes judgment on my own acts and states of mind, and pronounces some to be right and some to be wrong, he cannot restrain his contempt. And why? Because he evidently feels, as strongly as I do, that if there is a faculty which speaks of what *is* right or wrong, there must be one which speaks of that which *is* true and false. The faculties are clearly not identical; one has relation to me, to what *I* do and think: the other belongs to the region—I am afraid I must use the word—of the absolute. But there is so close an affinity between their processes, they blend so curiously and intricately, that it is scarcely possible for a man of logical and coherent mind, who is convinced of the non-existence of the (personal) judge, to recognize, for actual use, the existence of the general use. I must again affirm (notwithstanding Dr. Candlish's terrible sentence) that I suppose him and Mr. Mansel to use both these faculties every hour of their lives. All I mean is, that the non-recognition of a Reason which takes account of what which is, as distinct from what appears, involves the non-recognition of a Conscience which affirms this to be right for me and that to be wrong. I apprehend that the example of a reasoner like Mr. Mansel is the best answer to his question, what connection I discover between Kant's Reason with his three ideas and its corresponding paralogisms, and the doctrine of a Conscience as it is expounded in Butler's three Sermons. I should say that the difference between the character of the men, their countries, their forms of thought, makes it all the more remarkable that they should have arrived at conclusions which, being seemingly diverse, have this great test of internal sympathy and accordance, that you can scarcely reject the one without making light of the other.

I count it indeed a great advantage for England—one for which we ought to be thankful, though without assuming that what is best for us would have been best for Germany—that the inquiry respecting the Conscience is ours rather than the inquiry respecting the Reason, and that we cannot really avail ourselves of the second except through the first. Butler's sermons were, it seems to me, just what we needed, and that for two apparently opposite reasons. (1) They served to counteract the habit, which the Evangelical movement of that time was encouraging, of turning the experiences of evil in the minds of men into *laws* of their minds; in other words, of making the depravity of human nature the interpretation of human nature. (2) They justified all the appeals which the

Evangelical teachers were making to the Consciences of men, respecting their sins against God and their brethren,—appeals which their own theory did *not* justify,—appeals which the coldness of the school to which Butler belonged made impossible for them. And Butler's doctrine being brought to this test, its deficiency, and the cause of it, was also made manifest. When the preachers spoke of the Conviction of Sin, they assumed that GOD was speaking to the Conscience, that He was revealing to man his own moral condition. As I have hinted before, it seems to me that just this was wanted to make the idea of the Conscience a complete idea; and that in Butler it was inevitably incomplete, not from a fault in him, but because he was criticizing the mind of man from its own ground, not contemplating it from a higher ground. Looked at from this point of view, there are paralogisms and antinomies of the Conscience as there are of the Reason. He was partly aware of them; he had a sort of dialectic of his own for hindering the mischiefs that arise from them; but happily they did not lead him to treat the Conscience as "a faculty of lies;" happily they did not lead him to identify its decrees with the conclusions of the understanding from probable evidence; happily they did not discourage him from asserting in broad, even audacious language, its supremacy, leaving those who profited by his lessons to ascertain what is necessary to the real exercise of that supremacy.

Although, then, Butler was an avowed defender of the Bible, and Kant was suspected of undermining its authority, and of disputing a Revelation altogether, there was a curious resemblance between them, even in the point in which they at first sight seem to be most opposed. Butler, no doubt, appealed to texts, accepted them reverently, threw his inquiries into the form of discourses upon them. But he was to all intents and purposes as much a student of the facts of human nature, as much a careful critic of them, without seeking any interpretation but what was derived from themselves, as Kant was. And he was exposed to similar difficulties from that very cause. Each seemed to himself to have worked out a full explanation of the faculty he was conversant with, each really demanded further light to make its operation intelligible. And in due time each, it seems to me, gained that which it wanted, partly perhaps through the inquiries of philosophers and the teachings of divines, much more through the demands of the people.

If appeals to the *Conscience* became the characteristic of the new school of English preachers, the commencement of an age of *Reason* was hailed by the disciples of the new school in France. How little of sympathy there was between the first and Butler, I have hinted already. Surely there was no greater between the latter and the German. The glories of Reason had been sung by the Encyclopædists, who certainly were guiltless, if any men ever were, of looking beyond the limits of experience. Their phrases descended upon the mob of St. Antoine: certainly no association of the infinite and eternal was consciously mixed with them by the receivers. But they did undergo a mighty change in the new hands. Words which had represented to the philosophers of the salons the superiority of the few to the opinions and delusions of the many, represented to the multitude the overthrow of distinctions—and these, distinctions of intellect no less than of fortune and of birth. Here was the blind recognition of a human faculty, a faculty which does not set one above another, but which belongs to all. And here also, as Mr. Coleridge said in those papers of his which have been so much contemned and have exercised so much power, was an equally blind recognition of something, call it by what name you will, which passes the limits of experience, which is immeasurable, transcendent, universal. The name you find for that something may be Human Rights, or Humanity, may be a Brotherhood that breaks down all the boundaries of family and nation, may be this Reason itself. All these names will be tried; all have so much of meaning in them that numbers will adopt each, and consider that for a time all-sufficient. And those who do, if they find it necessary to cast down their god, and to say it is merely an idol, are in exceeding danger of becoming simple Atheists; perhaps in all the more danger if they agree to accept the traditions of their country because one tradition is not more false to them than another.

Do such observations strike you as very alarming,—excuses for the despondency into which we are all ready to fall? Very alarming, I think; but rather cures for desponding than excuses for it. Our forefathers of the last century learnt one lesson. They found there was something in every man which *might*, by God's mercy, be aroused, which *might* testify to him of his own rebellion. We want that assurance more than ever; there is great danger of our losing it. But to sustain it do we not want another? Is there not that in us all which does not merely belong to us as distinct individual beings, but which is common to us all, which is ours because we are members of a race? May not this too be spoken to? may not this too be called forth? Is not God speaking to it? is not God calling it forth? Is not this that to which He speaks when He reveals Himself to Man in the Son who took upon Him the nature of Man, who died for the whole human race? Is not this that spirit in us which He calls forth by His Spirit, which that Spirit teaches to say, Abba Father? If all Critical Philosophies, studies of the Absolute, French Revolutions, preaching of Rights, Humanity, Reason, are leading to this issue, can we mourn that they have been permitted or ordained? If they are not leading to this issue, may not we, the preachers of the Gospel, have ourselves to blame that when the gates of the Kingdom of Heaven are opening, we will not enter into them ourselves, nor suffer them who are entering to go in?

(4.) I have wandered not, I believe, from the proper text of this Letter, but far enough from the little personal questions which gave occasion to it. If I seem to return to them that I may notice Mr. Mansel's remarks on my very 'wonderful' uses of the faculty of Reason, and the illustration which he derives from my supposed intercourse with a Unitarian neighbour, I hope I shall be finding one more illustration of the principle for which I am contending, and shall not be betrayed into any angry defence of my own wisdom. If I am making wonderful uses of the faculty which all men possess, my folly and vanity must be capable of a much readier exposure—an appeal to the common judgment of men against me must be far more effectual—than if no such faculty exists. The assertion of such a possession for mankind is a witness against any idiosyncrasies of mine which I may try to pass over upon my fellow-creatures. Just so far as I appeal to it, I must be pointing to common objects, objects in which all alike are interested. I may, no doubt, practise tricks with it, as with any other faculty, availing myself of its own special illusions; but, if I hold that God Himself is revealing Himself to us that He may scatter illusions, I must hold that just so far as I proclaim Him to men, I am ensuring the exposure and scattering of my tricks.

With respect to my Unitarian neighbour, I maintain most assuredly that he has this faculty of Reason as much as I have. If I did not, and I yet held that the Trinity lay at the foundation of our human life, I should do my best by some arts of mine, and by force, if I had it at command, or could influence more powerful men to put it forth, to bring him over to my side, to impose my dogmas upon him. Because I am convinced that he has this faculty, and that God is speaking to it in him as in me, the more confidence I have in the honesty of his purposes and convictions, the more assured I shall be that he will be guided into all truth, the more gladly I shall help him to discover it. And the more assurance I have that the mystery of a Father, a Son, and a Spirit—three persons in One God—is the mystery in which we are living and moving and having our being, the more shall I be conscious that there are mists and illusions in my mind and heart as in his, which are keeping us from the full apprehension and enjoyment of that mystery, and the more shall I ask that whatever these are, He who knows us and loves us so inconceivably better than we know and love ourselves, will bring us into that light in which is no darkness at all. But we shall have more of this subject in a future letter.

Most truly yours,
F. D. M.

P.S. My friendly (and therefore faithful) critic in 'Fraser's Magazine' makes this observation on a passage in a subsequent Letter of mine respecting Kant:—

"In a subordinate matter we think he misappre-
"hends Mr. Mansel. The latter has used the fol-
"lowing expression:—'The object of which we are
"'conscious is thus, to adopt the well-known lan-
"'guage of the Kantian philosophy, a *phenomenon*,
"'not a *thing in itself*;' on which Mr. Maurice thus
"comments:—'I do not know why Mr. Mansel at-
"'tributes the distinction between a *phenomenon* and
"'*thing in itself* to the Kantian philosophy. It has
"'been a recognized distinction in every philosophy,
"'etc.'—*Maurice*, p. 333.

"If Mr. Maurice will look at Mr. Mansel's words
"again, he will see that they give no evidence of in-
"tention to attribute the distinction exclusively to
"the Kantian philosophy. But he who talks of the
"phenomenon and the thing in itself (*Ding an sich*),
"is undoubtedly adopting 'the well-known language'
"of that philosophy; he is using its peculiar termin-
"ology. Neither, on the other hand, while the dis-
"tinction is an integral part of the Kantian philo-
"sophy, is it admitted by every other. Mr. Mansel
"is therefore unfairly charged with 'imputing to
"'Kant specially what he has in common with half
"'the world;' and indeed the whole paragraph which
"thus winds up wants revision."

I willingly submit to this correction; but I think

the writer will perceive, when he has read this Letter, (1) why I was likely to be somewhat jealous in claiming the distinction of things as they are, and of phenomena as *not* a specially German distinction. (2) That I am as little inclined as any one can be to underrate the merits of Kant in giving fixedness to that distinction as one of the most important in Philosophy.*

---

* If I am not mistaken, the remark which I made, p. 178, respecting the effect of Coleridge upon later writers, who know very little of him, is borrowed from an observation of his own, perhaps in his Literary Life respecting Burke.

LETTER XI.

———

THE PRACTICAL REASON.—LOGIC UNDER DIFFERENT ASPECTS.—RULES AND PRINCIPLES.—TRUTH IN PROPOSITIONS AND IN A PERSON.

MY DEAR SIR,

If I do not make many extracts from the part of Mr. Mansel's 'Examination' which intervenes between p. 55 and p. 63, it is not that I wish to escape the humiliation of being represented to my readers as at once the most ignorant and the most arrogant of human beings. But as I have given already paragraph upon paragraph in which I appear in those characters, and as I do not find any very new or specific charge against me in these pages, I will simply ask that they may be read at full as they stand in the pamphlet. The tone which he has adopted may be a fitting punishment for my offences; it may draw upon me the ridicule of his admirers in Oxford or in the religious press. There are some students in Oxford, I believe, some religious men in different parts of England, who will not be hindered by it from seriously asking themselves whether his method of discussing the Infinite and the Absolute in his second Lecture was a right or a wrong one; whether the distinction between rules for practice, and principles that satisfy the Reason, which he sought to establish in the fifth Lecture was established or not; whether it was irreverent in me to speak of Christ as Himself the Truth, when I was considering his opinion that truth and falsehood are only properties of our conceptions. These are grave subjects, not quite settled by observations, however pointed and deserving of frequent repetition, about my brilliant discoveries or profound knowledge of philosophy. They will occupy me in this Letter.

(1.) When I read Mr. Mansel's second Lecture, I tried first to throw myself back into my undergraduate period, and to ask myself how I should have felt if I had heard it then. Next I considered how it must have affected any member of the classes which it was expressly designed to confute, whether they were Pantheists, or seekers for some moral foundation which was deeper than their own consciousnesses and conceptions. Such persons, it seemed to me, would not recognize the force of Mr. Mansel's logic at all as bearing upon themselves. They *would* recognize it as defining the nature of Christian Divinity, and as showing how little *it* met their wants. All reflections of this kind Mr. Mansel simply passes by. They do not touch him. He assumes that the thoughts that I have attributed to these people are imaginations of my own. Very poor and feeble, I confess that they are, in comparison of such statements of actual mental experience and mental suffering as are contained in Mr. Chretien's pamphlet. If the reader will meditate on that most serious narrative after he has amused himself with Mr. Mansel's lively criticisms on me, I shall not be at all afraid of any results that may follow from the latter. And there were many blanks in my statement which I ought not to have left at first; which at all events I should seek to fill up now.

1st. I may have led some of my readers to think that I did not recognize as strongly as Mr. Mansel does the difficulties and contradictions to which the Reason is exposed when it tries to grapple with the Absolute and the Eternal. My last Letter will have removed all suspicion from your mind on this point. I have shown you that I do confess these difficulties, and confess them to be inseparable from the independent exercise of the Reason. The question at issue between us are, whether these difficulties and contradictions are proofs that there is nothing in man which really demands a knowledge of the Infinite and Eternal, and that what seems to demand it is an impotency of the understanding, attempting unlawful and impossible flights; or whether these difficulties and contradictions only show that the faculty which God has given us for the apprehension can only put forth its full powers when He meets it and illuminates it. The practical treatment of the perplexities and contradictions that surround the study of the Infinite and the Absolute, and which have discovered finite and the Absolute, and which have discovered themselves in all investigations respecting that study, depends upon the answer to this question. If it is answered in the first way, Mr. Mansel's method of baffling and defeating the struggles of the mind after an object which it cannot reach, is the reasonable method. It is hard to charge the Lecturer with the vertigo and the sickness of heart which these experiments have caused in the listener or the reader. Granting that the maxim from which he started is right, he could not be hindered, by any dread of such painful effects, from administering the only medicine which could be effectual for the cure of the radical disease. But it is fair to ask whether these effects are not some evidence against the principle which forces the most skilful practitioners to adopt such a process of cure.

(2.) I hinted, and others have made the same observation, that there was a special incongruity in these logical puzzles when they were introduced into a pulpit discourse. If this was a mere feeling or sentiment, it is entitled to some weight, but not much. 'You do not,' Mr. Mansel might say, 'object to 'Butler's Sermons on Human Nature. Yet you 'confess that they are philosophical inquiries taking 'the form of Sermons. The form may not be the 'best possible, but you would rather have the thoughts 'in that form than not have them at all.' Certainly I would. I should indeed be sorry to see any

o

imitation of Butler's sermons in this day; first, because I think it would be a poor one; secondly, because I believe that the idea of Sermons, as meant to convey a Gospel from God to men, not an inquiry about God,—starting from the human ground,—has established itself among us since his time, and that it is a sound idea, which for many reasons we cannot afford to part with, which requires to be expanded and developed, not in any way resisted. But subject to that observation, we should be thankful that Butler made this great addition to our literature, without curiously considering whether it might have been better made in the shape of an Essay, like his Analogy. But here is the difference. Butler is investigating the conditions of human nature, without any especial reference to the Divine Nature. The Bampton Lecturer is investigating the conditions of human nature, especially as they bear upon its capacity of knowing the Divine. And the moment he comes in contact with that Divine Nature, he exclaims, 'I 'count it more reverent not to speak of that by its 'own proper name. I would rather talk of the Infi-'nite or of the Absolute than of GOD.' *Here* lay the contradiction, and it was the sense of this contradiction, not a merely æsthetic feeling about the sacredness of a church or the conditions of a sermon, which caused the revulsion which I and so many have felt. The preacher, the messenger from God, dares not assume that character. Evidently he is convinced that on his ground he ought not to assume it, and his readers bear an unconscious testimony, that there is truth in that conviction. But is not this an *experimentum crucis* of his position? He proposes to annihilate the philosophies of the Absolute for the sake of Divinity. That he may do it, he must abandon the very characteristic of a divine.

(3.) Herein, I conceive, lies the true difference between Sir William Hamilton and Mr. Mansel, which in my comments on his second Lecture I very imperfectly pointed out, but which has presented itself to me strongly since I have been called to review my book. The question whether the Infinite and the Absolute can be anything but negations of the finite and the conditioned, seemed to Hamilton, contemplating it as a logician, capable of but one answer. The philosophers of the Absolute did not shake him at all. He could dispose of them. But when those words of Manilius and of Prosper occurred to him, which speak of man as in some sense percipient of God, he hesitated; there was something awful there; he would rather contradict himself than dispute such language. It is *such* language that Mr. Mansel, if he is to carry Sir William Hamilton's doctrine into the region of Theology, has to encounter. He has a reverence for the Name; the idea, before which the philosopher stood appalled, the English divine is pledged to grapple with. The perception of the Infinite and the Absolute means, in his Lectures, the perception of God. And he is precluded from saying,

'That which you are feeling after and cannot find,
' I can declare to you.' He is precluded from saying,
' You only arrive by your logic at a negative infinite.
' The Positive Infinite reveals Himself to you as He
' is.' These are the very statements which he rejects,
and undertakes to confute. In the interest of Divinity he is to renounce a principle which Sir William
Hamilton, speaking only as a philosopher, was ready,
almost in words, certainly in fact, to concede.

(4.) My most friendly critics have suspected that I
intended to disparage Logic, when I spoke in my notice of this Lecture, and other Lectures of Mr. Mansel, concerning the use which he makes of Logic. I
must have spoken very unadvisedly if I led any one
to suspect me of such folly. What I feel and have
always felt is, that there is a Logic of the Understanding, which deserves all honour whilst it confines
itself within its own limits, and contents itself with
telling us under what laws and in what forms we
must discourse. That there is a higher Dialectic, a
Logic belonging to that Faculty which converses with
the Infinite and the Absolute, Kant maintained, and
endeavoured to discover what that Dialectic was.
There has also been a very vigorous attempt, in all
ages, to construct a Dialectic of the Conscience; innumerable books of Casuistry have been and are the
fruits of that effort. Believing that Kant deprived
the Reason of its proper complement, so far as he
did not accept a Revelation, I must suppose that his

Dialectic of the Reason may be very instructive, and must be imperfect. Believing that God illuminates the Consciences of all men, I must hold that the dialectic of the Casuists is more than negatively defective, is often positively mischievous, inasmuch as it becomes itself, or it makes the priest, an opaque medium for obstructing the light, a barrier between the Spirit of God and the Spirit of man. But I cannot therefore say that there is not a real Dialectic for the Reason as well as one for the Conscience. On the contrary, it seems to me now that the more light I gain from the Bible, illustrated by human history, respecting the Divine Revelation to the race, the nearer I approach to the Dialectic for the Reason. And the more light I gain from the Bible, illustrated by personal experience and human biographies, concerning the Revelation to the individual, the nearer I approach to a Dialectic for the Conscience. In the attempt to organize the one or the other, we fall into the continual temptation of substituting private interpretations and the opinions of our age, for that which is actually told us either in books or in life. The discovery of our own rash conclusions, and of those of others, *may* lead us to think that there are no laws governing us in one direction or other—in the region of the finite or of the Infinite—or no one who can interpret those laws for us. The despair is greatest, I think, if we are *only* conversant with the finite, if we suppose that all we can know is to be learnt from it. The despair is least if we believe there is an Infinite Spirit of Truth watching over every faculty and over all its movements, enabling it to find out its own functions and the end of its existence—its own special temptations and dangers; enabling it to reverence the acts and exercises of every other. For then we may be sure that the accumulated experiences of ages, of all earnest study and discovery, of all errors and confusions, must be tending to the same end. And each person may say for himself, 'That Spirit would 'guide me into all truth; would show me all that leads 'me to be false, and would save me from it—from my 'fanaticism, and my indifference, from the special be- 'wilderments of the Reason, of the Conscience, and 'of the Understanding; from those more complicated 'bewilderments which arise when each forgets its 'place, and imposes its laws upon the other.' It is this imposition of the Logic of the Understanding upon the Conscience and the Reason, arising from a disbelief in their distinct objects and obligations, which I think we are bound to resist to the utmost. It was against this I spoke; not against any application of what is taught as Logic in Oxford, within its own sphere. While it works within that sphere, all ought to pay it reverence; if it attempts its old usurpations, the Theologian, the Moralist, the Mathematician, the Physical Student, must once more enter into conspiracy to secure their proper freedom.

II. A question of deeper and of more evident interest to mankind is hidden behind this. The distinction which Kant draws between the Speculative and Practical Reason was alluded to in the last Letter. Evidently Mr. Mansel's distinction between Speculative and Regulative truths has *some* relation to this; he is as anxious as those who more nearly agree with Kant can be, that they shall not be supposed to be the same. Kant having affirmed that there is that in us which takes cognizance of the Infinite and Eternal, could not confound this faculty with that in us which confesses an obligation to do something or to be something. But on the other hand, he could not help saying that if we analyze that sense of obligation, it will be found at last to do homage, not to changeable, or finite, or partial, but to eternal, infinite, universal laws. Looking at the subject simply as a critic of our faculties he could only consider these as laws in or of the Reason itself; whatever imperfections are involved in that mode of contemplating them seem to be inseparable from his course of investigation. Distinct from this subject, but yet lying so close to it that they cannot in practice be separated, is that which refers to the power and operation of these laws. Do they bind us by an iron chain of necessity? Or are they by their very nature such as speak to the Will, such as can be disobeyed?

Supposing a person to deny the existence of a faculty which apprehends the Eternal and Infinite, and to admit the sense in us of obligation, some such division as that which Mr. Mansel has developed in these Lectures, is inevitable. There must be that which answers to the Speculative Reason. And seeing that the subjects of it are not the Infinite and the Eternal—seeing that these are cut off as not subjects of human thought at all—we are forced to ask, *What* has that speculative faculty to do? what are the truths with which it comes in contact? There must again be some faculty which answers to the Practical Reason, some faculty which confesses obligation; and seeing that this cannot apprehend laws that are eternal and universal, we are forced to ask, What has *this* faculty to do? *what* obligations does it own; to what and by what does it affirm that we are bound?

I must beg you to observe how these inquiries become complicated with that which I endeavoured to bring before my readers. Supposing Kant to be right in saying that man has a faculty which demands the Eternal,—supposing him to be also right in saying that he has a faculty which confesses an obligation to some Eternal, Universal Law or Principle,—a Revelation of God might satisfy the Speculative Reason by discovering the Eternal which is demanded; or it might satisfy the practical Reason by declaring what law or principle it is which we are formed to obey. It might do *either* of these things: might it not do both? *Must* it not do both if it is such a Revelation as the Bible sets forth to us? If it is the Revelation of a Moral Being,—of a Being of Truth, Goodness, Justice, Mercy,—is the faculty which demands the Infinite and Eternal and Absolute discontented ? Would it say, 'I do not want this, but only the ' name or notion of what is infinite, absolute, eternal' ? Would it not say, 'Yes; Truth, Goodness, Justice, ' are exactly what cannot be brought under the laws ' of space and time, what defy all kinds of finite mea-' surement' ? But what would the practical Reason say to such a discovery? Would it not say, 'Yes; here ' are those principles of Justice, Goodness, Truth, ' which constitute my obligation to be true and good ' and just. Outward laws imposing penalties for acts ' which imply a departure from Truth, Goodness, Jus-' tice, must have issued from the Mind in which these ' dwell absolutely, eternally, infinitely. And that ' Mind, just because it is eternal, absolute, infinite, ' may be at once the standard of mine and of the ' minds of all men, and may act upon us to mould us ' into conformity with itself' ? In this way those two faculties or perceptions, which are necessarily diverse, and appear sometimes as if they could not well be brought into harmony when they are looked at as faculties of ours, become united and harmonize by that light which falls upon them from above. Each finds that which meets its own need. The man in whom they dwell is no longer a dislocated being, no longer a mere philosophical compound; he is a living unity. And so also that other problem, insoluble when it is looked at upon the human ground, receives a Divine solution. The absolute and perfect Will, the Will to all good, has its highest throne over the will of man, which is formed in its image. Its laws are laws not for stones and animals, but for creatures that can trust, hope, love; and may sink into distrust, despair, hatred; which by the influence of the Divine may be raised out of the devilish, or be preserved from sinking into it.

But supposing there be no speculative Reason and no practical, in Kant's sense of those words, the inquiry must be pressed which I have suggested: What are the speculative truths which it is possible for man to perceive? What are those regulative truths which may affect his conduct? Mr. Chretien has pursued the first of these inquiries with a clearness, an earnestness, and a subtlety, which leave nothing to desire. I only hope that his argument will not be felt by any Oxford reader merely to bear upon Mr. Mansel,—merely to show that the logic of a great logician has in a special instance failed. The Bampton Lecturer, it appears to me, has done an infinite service to us all, by showing that a denial, which is common to him with three-fourths of English psychologists, and probably of English divines, involves the contradiction which Mr. Chretien has pointed out. Admit nothing but a faculty of the understanding, and the question, 'Where are your speculative truths? are they not mere 'generalizations from objects that are presented to 'your senses?' must strike us the more we reflect. And the difficulty becomes enormously increased by that which we might hope would relieve it, the belief that God has spoken to His creatures, that He has told them anything about Himself. The question which Mr. Chretien has felt to be so tremendous, 'Can the 'true God tell us about Himself what is not true? will recur at every step. By introducing a revelation upon that hypothesis, you confuse the whole idea of truth and falsehood more than ever in our minds.

But though I felt this difficulty very strongly, I felt that which is connected with the other part of the division more strongly still. We want regulative truths. Who does not feel that we want them? Truths to regulate and govern our whole lives, truths to determine our thoughts and our conduct, truths to act upon us at every moment of our lives, truths that can raise us out of falsehood and evil. I asked Mr. Mansel to tell us where these truths were to be had, let what would happen to those other speculative truths. I found him answering, that "In religion, " in morals, in our daily business, in the care of our " lives, in the exercise of our senses, the rules which " guide our practice cannot be reduced to principles " which satisfy our reason." I fancied that this was an appeal to experience and fact. Those questions which have puzzled metaphysicians, and lie out of the high-road of common life, might be tried by what is passing in common life. I thought that when

Mr. Mansel spoke of the exercise of our senses, he meant the exercise of hearing, seeing, smelling, tasting, handling. I thought when he spoke of daily business, he meant the things which ordinary men are busy about every day. Following this analogy, I thought that by Religion and Morals he meant that which we commonly understand by those words when we use them in their simplest sense; and that by the care of our lives, he meant the watching against colds and fevers and rheumatism. Such homely, practical illustrations seemed to me exceedingly worthy of a philosopher who esteemed regulative above speculative truths. I could not conceive a better way of arriving at a safe judgment upon the question what was required for our practical guidance, than that which he suggested. I therefore followed him implicitly, trying to ascertain, in each of these particulars, whether those whom he as well as I would esteem the most practical and wise people were seeking for rules or for principles. If it appeared that in the very commonest events and experiences rules are found inefficient, principles are demanded, one might suppose this was *à fortiori* true in the higher region of thought. But it appears that I offered the grossest insult to Mr. Mansel in assuming that he meant what his words expressed. Hear how he speaks.

"Was ever such egregious trifling solemnly pro-
"claimed under the name of an argument? What
"on earth any one of these propositions has to do

"with anything asserted or denied in the Bampton
"Lectures,—what conceivable connection exists be-
"tween 'anatomical and physiological principles' or
"'the laws which our senses follow in their work-
"'ings,' and the problems above cited as insoluble—
"is a secret which lies hidden in the unfathomable
"depths of Mr. Maurice's association of ideas. To
"attempt a serious refutation of such reasoning would
"be to insult the understanding of the reader."—
(*Examination*, pp. 60, 61.)

I perfectly admit Mr. Mansel's right to say, 'I, an
'Oxford Professor, speak only of Kings and Tetrarchs,
'of all great things, of "Liberty and Necessity, Per-
'"sonality and Reality, the One and the Many,"'
etc.; but if he *does* allude to the exercise of the
senses and so forth, are we poor Londoners very in-
excusable for flattering ourselves that he has, for the
moment, descended to our level; that he is willing
to make himself intelligible to us through 'things
with which we are familiar? Not that I have even
the slightest cause of complaint. Any disputant
would bear the sharpest scoffs and taunts, if he could
see his opponent withdrawing from the open field he
had chosen himself, and confessing that he was only
safe in heights and thickets. But for one who believes, as I do, that the distinction of the speculative
truths and regulative truths in the form which Mr.
Mansel has stated it, is likely to shut out the sun
over our heads and the ground at our feet, nothing
can be so satisfactory as that he should make this

confession to plain persons, that at all events it is not for them, that it may serve very well in the schools, that it has not even the slightest relation to the life of man.

III. We are prepared now for the last of the subjects I proposed to discuss in this Letter. " Truth and " Falsehood," Mr. Mansel said in his Lectures, " are " not properties of things in themselves, but of our " conceptions." I found fault with this statement. I quoted in connection with it the words, " I am the " Truth." Several of my critics, otherwise favourably disposed to me, have remonstrated with me on the injustice of treating this doctrine respecting Truth as if it belonged expressly to the Bampton Lecturer. They have reminded me that it may be found, or something equivalent to it, in almost every treatise on Logic. Mr. Mansel is not so much astonished at my injustice, —that of course he expected from me,—as frightened at my irreverence. That I should venture to introduce so sacred a text into a discussion of this kind, appears to him very shocking.

I am not the least inclined to dispose of these objections lightly. They are entitled to the gravest consideration, for their own sake and for the principles which are involved in them. I will begin with the first.

1. Supposing there is only a Logic for the Understanding—only that Logic which the most eminent English writers undertake to expound, I grant at once

that Truth is only concerned with Propositions; and that Propositions are concerned with our conceptions, not with things as they are. If therefore a writer on formal Logic—taken in that sense in which alone he wishes it to be taken—defines Truth and Falsehood as Mr. Mansel describes them, I should see no ground for remonstrating. I should consider the question an open one whether that was the only Logic. I should reserve a right to recognize Truth in quite another sense—and to hold that as the highest and the simplest. But I should not obtrude that sense, where it was not appropriate; or deny that one which had been given where it was appropriate.

You will understand me when I say that I could not quite adopt this course when I read that very remarkable book of our times, Mr. Mill's Logic. Just because it was so much more comprehensive, more exhaustive, than other treatises of the same kind,— just because it was impossible to doubt that he had considered every subject which he handled, not merely as a technical dialectician, but as a psychologist and metaphysician,—just because Kant was as well known to him as Locke, and the old Schoolmen as either,— it was not possible for one feeling as I do, not to be more disturbed when I found *him* speaking of Truth as having only to do with propositions, than when the same sentiment came from one who more strictly confined himself within the formal limits. I remember writing down in my copy of his Logic, when it first appeared, words which indicated how bitterly I felt the separation which that part of his work seemed to establish between my thoughts and those of a man for whom I had the greatest admiration. His recent work on 'Liberty,' in which I should probably find more 'propositions' to dissent from than in the Logic, caused me great delight, because it seemed to bridge over this chasm,—convincing me that in his heart of hearts the author acknowledges a substantial truth which is above all propositions—for which it is worth while to fight and suffer and die. But however I may have lamented that the intellectual doctrine of the Logic should have such an advocate,—however gladly I may have accepted this moral counteraction of it,—I should have considered it altogether unjust, immoral, and irreverent, to introduce our Lord's words, "I am the Truth," into an argument with Mr. Mill. If I had done so, I should have made a shameful appeal to popular feeling in a question which he had submitted to philosophical reasoning; I should be subjecting him to a test which he had not accepted, and was not the least bound to accept; I should lay myself open to the unanswerable retort, 'Are you sure that your most 'orthodox divines adopt those words in the sense you 'put upon them?'

I give you this instance in order that you may compare it with the one before us. I was not criticizing a treatise on Logic, but a volume of Sermons. The preacher of those Sermons was employed in confuting all who set aside the authority of the Bible. He called upon the young men whom he addressed to accept it altogether or reject it altogether. The very question at issue between me and the writer of those Sermons was about the nature of Speculative and Regulative Truth; whether they can be distinguished, *what* is the distinction, whether Truth itself does not vanish if it is such as he tried to make it. If the preacher was allowed to take for granted the definition of Truth which belongs to formal Logic, everything was taken for granted; there was no room for further disputation; all the negative part of his doctrine was established. Had I not a right, then, to turn upon him, and say, 'But how does this consist ' with the positive statements which you not only hold ' yourself but censure others for not holding? Is this ' the account of Truth which is given in the book ' that we are to receive altogether or not at all? Do ' these words, "I am the Truth," mean anything or ' nothing?'

Mr. Mansel hints that my allusion to English feelings about these words was very little to the purpose. It would have had a purpose, but in my judgment a very wrong purpose, if I had called in the English reverence for Scripture to overwhelm any person who was arguing a scientific question, either respecting Logic or Physics. I know not which are injured most by such appeals, the man of science,

P

or they whose aid is invoked to crush him. He is taught that the Bible has some interest which is unfavourable to the investigation of Truth; they are taught to regard the Bible not as a book which is to make them true, but to prove other men false.

But I maintain that the allusion to English feeling had an obvious and a legitimate purpose in a book which was expressly written to show that a method which was adopted to kill German Rationalism, and to preserve English faith, might prove fatal to it. I maintain that that allusion was demanded, since, as I fear, the reverence for Truth, in the ordinary and practical transactions of life, is growing less amongst us, and will perish altogether if the relation between that truth and the highest Truth is taken to be a mere imaginary and artificial one; if the common name being retained, it is supposed to represent the most diverse and heterogeneous senses. And this conviction, which I held very strongly before, has been much deepened in me by Mr. Mansel's second objection to me.

2. It is very irreverent to introduce the words which Christ spoke at the Passover Supper into such a discussion as this. I do not the least object to the form in which this accusation is brought; the ruder and coarser the setting is, the more suitable it is to the sentiment which it encloses. That sentiment I solemnly submit to the consideration of all thoughtful people, especially of all Oxford teachers and students.

It is come to this; Christ's words are to be received, because they are written in the book which we call the Bible. But those words which have been most felt to meet the want of human beings,—those which have been quoted again and again in sermons as *the* answer to the question which Pilate would not wait to have answered,—those which have been the comfort to thousands of weary inquirers after Truth, who could find no rest in any propositions or any conclusions of their own understandings,—those are not to be allowed to mingle with any of our common thoughts, not even with any of our deepest speculations. The truth which Mr. Mansel speaks of in the schools, the truth which we are to utter with our lips in the market-place, is altogether apart from this Truth; it is a sin to associate them. When I said that I believed the function of the preacher was obsolete if he had no right to proclaim an eternal truth to men, or if men had no faculty for receiving it, I was answered, 'Oh, the Bampton Lecturer is 'only withdrawing us from that which is past finding 'out, that he may fix our minds on that which has 'been brought nigh to us in Christ. He would not 'have us explore the abysses; he would have us con-'template the Person in whom the Truth has taken a 'living form.' Again and again I have been charged with unfairness and blindness for not perceiving that this was the scope and intent of the Lectures. Here is my defence, made for me by Mr. Mansel himself.

If any language expresses the coming forth of that which was hidden into manifestation, that it may become a portion and treasure for human beings, the answer to Thomas expresses it. And this answer is what must not be exhibited in relation with human thoughts, experiences, judgments, acts!

This being the acknowledged principle of Mr. Mansel, had I not some cause to ask, What then *is* Revelation?

Very truly yours,
F. D. M.

LETTER XII.

THE UNITARIAN CONTROVERSY.

My dear Sir,

Pages 63-73 of the 'Examination' are occupied with the Unitarian Controversy. They are introduced by the following remarks :—

"Mr. Maurice commences his ninth Letter with a
" dissertation on the 'controversy respecting the Many
" ' and the One ;' which he tells us ' has been a wea-
" ' risome enough controversy in the schools ;' but
" which, as he has now discovered, also ' expresses a
" ' profound difficulty to the wayfarer ;' and the dis-
" cussion of which by philosophers, he thinks, ' should
" ' be welcomed as a proof that they are coming into
" ' contact with our actual necessities, and that they
" ' cannot merely think and speak as Schoolmen.'
" Let us pause at this sentence, to go back a few
" pages. A short time ago, the Schoolmen were de-
" scribed by Mr. Maurice as ' a set of very earnest
" ' men,' in whose conflict ' we may discover true
" ' principles which do not belong to the schools, but
" ' to mankind.' A short time ago, the problem of

"the Many and the One, with others of the same "kind, was classed among 'nuts for children to crack' "and 'conundrums for breakfast-parties.' The critic "now reverses his judgment in both cases. The "Schoolmen are thinkers and speakers who cannot "'come into contact with our actual necessities:' the "' nuts for children to crack' have become 'profound "'difficulties to the wayfarer.' Why does Mr. Mau- "rice thus blow hot and cold with the same breath? "Simply, as it seems, because it is convenient to "praise or vilify the Schoolmen, according as he "thinks he can discover in them an unlikeness or a "likeness to the Bampton Lecturer.

"We shall see a few pages later why Mr. Maurice "changes his tone concerning the Schoolmen. It is "preparatory to calling his antagonist 'a Schoolman.' "The epithet is meant to be insulting: but perhaps "the object of this withering sarcasm may be satisfied "with the reply of Bishop Horsley on a similar oc- "casion to Dr. Priestley. 'Perhaps, Sir, though a "'Protestant divine, I may sometimes condescend to "'look into the *Summa,* and may be less mortified "'than you conceive with this comparison. It was "'well meant, however, and is one of those general "'depreciatory insinuations which are apt to catch "'the vulgar, and may serve the purpose of a reply, "'upon any occasion when a real reply is not to be "'found.' Mr. Maurice seems fully aware of the ad- "vantage to be derived from such 'general deprecia-

"'tory insinuations.' 'This Oxford schoolman,' he
" says, ' urges us to accept a certain theological tenet
" ' respecting the Being we worship, because we really
" ' can know nothing of Him; because as He is Infi-
" ' nite, and we finite, it is impossible for us to say
" ' that this representation of Him may not be as near
" ' the truth as any other. Certainly there was need
" ' of persecution or bribes to persuade people of the
" ' duty of accepting a doctrine which by the showing
" ' of its defender could attach itself to no deep or in-
" ' ward conviction! If bribes and persecution should
" ' both fail, what will become of it?' The doctrine
" of which he is speaking is that of the Holy Trinity."
—(*Examination*, pp. 63–65.)

You will be struck with the harmony between this passage and all that have preceded it. Mr. Mansel thinks that I have been guilty of an inconsistency in my way of speaking of the Schoolmen. He can account for it at once. I meant to call him a schoolman, therefore I changed my tone and disparaged those whom I had praised. No other motive occurred to him as possible but this; having discovered this, the contradiction itself naturally looked a little more flagrant than perhaps it was. You, who will not suspect me of simply belying all my convictions for the sake of libelling an opponent whom I do not know, and towards whom I had not the slightest excuse for entertaining a dislike, will perhaps allow me to explain what I did say about the Schoolmen, and this question of the Many and the One. It will be the best preparation for the important subject that follows, in treating which I hope I may, in one sense, lose sight of what is personal; there is a sense in which no one would less expect or wish me to sever personality from that subject than yourself.

I cannot feel the point of the quotation from Bishop Horsley's answer to Dr. Priestley as keenly as Mr. Mansel intended that I should, seeing that I also am guilty of often referring to the *Summa*, and have derived great instruction from it. I have expressed, in the book to which I alluded before, as much admiration of the powers of Aquinas as I think Bishop Horsley can have felt. Nor have I concealed my opinion that the less popular opponent of his school, Duns Scotus, the ultra-realist, the defender of the immaculate conception of the Virgin, is entitled to his own honour. In these discussions, often described as barren and obsolete, I have found what I think fruitful hints respecting the perplexities of our time. If later study has pointed out great errors in the school method, I suspect that we are liable to fall into those errors in spite of the warning. As sign-posts to many tracks of thought into which we must travel, as beacons to keep us from some paths in which we may lose ourselves, the Schoolmen appear to me most valuable for all who have leisure to consult them.

At the same time, I cannot dissent from the opinion which all men express, in one language or another, that we are fallen upon an age as unlike as possible that in which the Schoolmen lived,—an age of Newspapers, an age in which all thought takes popular forms; an age in which not only every divine, but every metaphysician, almost every logician, is trying to make himself heard by common men and women. How to behave ourselves in this age must be a great and difficult question for us all. Warnings we hear from all sides against the popular Scylla where all knowledge is made easy, against the Charybdis of antiquarian lore, which no one can be interested in. But how to steer between them, this is what we learn, I suppose, not much from charts or pilots,—chiefly from our own flounderings and shipwrecks. As I have spoken on this subject in my second Letter, and have referred to it so often since, I will not trouble you with any narrative of my own adventures and mistakes. I will simply repeat the result. It has been a conviction that the Schoolmen were occupied in most earnest inquiries; that these inquiries had always a tendency to become verbal and merely notional; that, as John of Salisbury and others among them complained, this tendency sometimes became dominant over every other; that even the verbal discussions were not without the greatest use as leading to the formation of an accurate nomenclature, and still more as discovering their own inadequacy; that beneath them lay eternal principles which they could not comprehend in their formulas, which they did not possess, but which possessed them, to which they paid inward homage, and which really gave them their interest in their controversies, and accounted for that which seems to us a zeal about trifles; that it is the calling of our time to bring out these principles and present them to our fellow-men, not as dogmatic conditions of the understanding, but as the grounds of their lives; that if we do not recognize this vocation, and fulfil it, we shall combine all the evils of the scholastic with all the evils of the popular temper; that then we shall produce a compound that may be accepted both in halls of learning and by the reading public, and which will be equally injurious to both.

The instance of this danger which I am about to consider is a very striking one. The religious public are troubled with the presence of persons who deny the doctrine of the Trinity as it is set forth in our Creeds. They know some general answers to the arguments of these persons which are collected out of the Bible and are summed up in tracts. But they want some that are more philosophical, some that they can produce with triumph when the opponent says that they are holding an irrational tenet. These they expect the Universities to supply. The task is undertaken. They are told that the controversy about the Many and the One is a very old controversy; that it has been carried on as much among philosophers as among divines; that the first have been as little able to obtain any satisfaction upon it as the last; that it is in fact impossible to advance many steps in such inquiries; that there is darkness before and behind; that the human mind is overreaching its own limits when it tries to penetrate the darkness. Is not this just what the orthodox disputant wants? Has he not a prescription, drawn out in the most learned terms of art, for silencing the Unitarian doubters?

Now I venture to think that this is not a mode of repelling Anti-Trinitarians or of defending the Trinity which could the least have satisfied any one of the old Schoolmen. The Trinity was associated in their minds with the Beatific Vision, with the beholding of God. If that language was especially adopted by the more mystical of their body, it was never wanting in the most intellectual. It was the real ground of Anselm's opposition to Rosellinus; it stirred up Bernard's indignation against Abelard; it was at the bottom of the teaching of the Master of Sentences; it was found in the Angelic Doctor no less than in the Seraphic. There might be various degrees of subtlety in different defences of the Creeds' against those who were suspected of different forms of Heresy. But in the minds of all there was the recognition of a Mystery in which they were living and moving and having their being, a Mystery which alone gave worth and interest to their dogmatic distinctions and to their argumentative feats. If they were often unjust to the intellectual difficulties of their opponents, as I conceive Bernard was to Abelard's, the excuse which they made to themselves was that a truth in which all men alike were interested, the truth which lay at the very foundation of the Church, was put in hazard by the dialectical dexterity of particular minds. Here, too, was the plea for silencing the disputants, by the general authority of the Church,—though reasoning was nearly always thrown in to help authority. The evidence of that authority, where it rested, how it could be ascertained, might be often feeble enough; but the assurance that the principle itself was a universal one, one in which all had an interest, had a probative force,—as Mr. Bentham would say,—not only for the Laity but for the Doctors, which did not dwell in any decrees of Popes or testimonies of Antiquity. Yes! in that period which was emphatically the period for defending Dogmas,—for perfecting a logical nomenclature suitable to all studies, to Theology especially,—for arguing out points of the most curious refinement, —there was, at the root of all this, the confession of an Eternal Substance and Unity which sustained the child and the hoary elder, of which the Doctor and the Peasant might have fruition together.

If we look at the subject from the other side, I maintain that there is a popular belief in the Trinity which may need strengthening, but which can derive no strength, only weakness, from those clever arguments with which it is supplied for the demolition of its adversaries. I mean the faith in a Father who has created, in a Son who has redeemed, in a Holy Ghost who sanctifies. Many questions arise in the minds of those who hold this faith; often it is obscured on one side or the other. But it is strongest in acts of Prayer; it is realized when the man actually arises and goes to his Father; when the thought of his own slavery or of that of others, drives him to a Redeemer; when he feels the need of One to encounter his corruptions, to guide him out of darkness into light, out of tumult into peace. If he hears that there are any who would take from him what he finds so near and dear to him, —and if, having contemplated the subject chiefly in reference to himself, he is not at all ready at discovering general arguments,—he may no doubt be glad to clutch at any which are thrown in his way, not much caring to investigate their nature. But when he does look into them, what a contrast do they offer to all that he prizes most! He is to tell his Unitarian neighbour that he has no right to reject probable evidence, the opinions of centuries, the traditional interpretations of Scripture, because all the paths in divinity are so dark and trackless, that no certainty is to be had. Whereas he longs to tell that neighbour,—and when he is left to his own instincts he does tell him,— that what they both want is certainty; that for himself he cannot be content without it; that he finds uncertainty when he looks out upon the world, but that he turns to God as the rest from this uncertainty, as the guide through it; that when he says 'Our Father,' it is an actual Father to whom he is speaking, and who is beckoning him home; that he knows that Father because He speaks to him through a Son;

that a Spirit of love and power, and a sound mind, which he is sure is not his own, enables him to claim his sonship and his heritage. These may be very poor arguments; the most ordinary Logician of the Understanding can expose their assumptions. Nevertheless, Logic does not reach them or deprive them of their power. That they only lose when the fervent speaker tries to piece them out with a lore which he has learnt from others; then the old garment and the new make a curious mixture, and the rents become painfully visible.

Any one observing the effect which such statements as these produce on numbers upon whom arguments either fall dead, or whom they only awaken to hostility, is inclined to speak much of the force of *Conviction*. A man thoroughly persuaded of the faith he holds, it is said, can do wonders, while the most practised fencer can do nothing. Mr. Mansel is right in supposing that I attached great weight to the force of Conviction; but he is quite wrong in supposing that I opposed it to *Dogmas*. I entirely agree with him that a man must be convinced of something, and that that something, not the conviction, is what we must set forth to our fellow-men. The question between us is, whether that is my Dogma or the Being about whom I hold the Dogma. If I believe in the Trinity, I believe in the Father, the Son, and the Holy Ghost, the one God blessed for ever. I believe in a Living God. But if so, surely to speak of Him is better than to speak of my notions about Him;

or even of my convictions, which will be feeble or vital in proportion as they are or are not divorced from that which calls them forth. In using this language, I am departing very widely from Mr. Mansel's teaching, but I am not setting up any counter-teaching of my own. I am in harmony both with the highest faith of the Schoolmen as I have just described it, and with the most earnest faith of doers and sufferers in the world. The Trinity was to the first the Infinite Charity, the Absolute Truth and Goodness, the Mystery that is about us, which we behold most imperfectly now, which the glorified saints see eye to eye. The others, dwelling less in this transcendent Unity, often losing sight of it altogether, are led by different conflicts and torments of their own mind to the perception of each distinct Person as having a demand on their trust and confidence; as the ground of their thoughts and acts. The one were professional Dogmatists, occupied with all Ecclesiastical speculations; here was the pillar of their souls; here was that which gave their dreary debates their significance. The others are always perplexed when the Unitarian tells them that God cares about life and not Dogmas; there is so much in their own hearts which answers to the sentiment; they repel it by tears, not words; they are sure what they mean is not a Dogma; if it only be an opinion of theirs or of all men, they know it must go to pieces. They believe it is of God, and they can ask Him to take care of it.

To me it seems that this is a very sound confidence, one which a believer in the Trinity ought to entertain if there were no experience to sustain it, one which is actually confirmed by the most clear warrants of experience. This article in Mr. Mansel's 'Examination' suggests some of the most remarkable. He says, that my language respecting Dogmas does not strike at him more than at Bull, Waterland, Horsley, at the most eminent English divines who have taken part in the Trinitarian controversy. All have brought their learning to bear upon the support of a Dogma; all have contended against the impugners of a Dogma. I admit the assertion, subject to certain qualifications. Neither Bull, nor Waterland, nor Horsley, is *merely* the champion of a Dogma. Each, as a learned man, introduces a vast amount of history into the discussion; each actually sets forth something of the mind of the age from which his authorities are drawn, something of the mind of the individual fathers and schoolmen to whom he refers. Each is obliged to investigate a large province of thought, and the origin and force of words which have been used by generations of men. Such inquiries must not be confounded with the mere defence of an opinion, or the confutation of an opinion; they have a distinct substantive worth; they illustrate, partially of course, but they *do* illustrate, long acts in the divine drama. Often their opponents may also have thrown light on these acts, may have suggested hints which *they* did not suggest; with less erudition,

LETTER XII. 225

may have yet opened historical paths which later philologers may be able to connect with those from which they appear most widely to diverge. But if one could forget these great accessories to their refutations, and regard them simply as controversialists, the question must force itself upon us, 'What has all their learn-'ing and ability effected? What opponents did they 'in their lifetime, or do they now convince? How 'many earnest believers in the Trinity can say, "We "'trace our establishment in that belief chiefly to these "'triumphant exposures of Unitarian fallacies or mis-"'takes"?' There may be such. It is no evidence that there are not that I have never met with them or heard of them. But I think I have met with some and heard of more who have gathered an impression from these controversies, that a doctrine which required so much clever reasoning to support it, so much acute and not always satisfactory criticism of words and constructions, could not be of much real importance to mankind, might be safely left to the judgment of scholars. I think I have met with some clergymen, and heard of more, who have suffered not a little in their own minds, and in their influence over their flocks, from having fitted themselves out with an armoury of evidences against Anti-Trinitarianism taken from those accomplished writers; so that they have seemed even to themselves to change positions with their adversaries, to be maintaining a negative instead of a positive, and have left the feeling upon the

Q

hearts of those who heard or read their discourses, that what they were pleading for must be altogether unlike that which was set forth in the Creeds for the life and health of the Christian man.

Surely the pious belief that God will take care of any truth better than we can take care of it, derives support from these facts. There are others which you know as well as I do, that point in the same direction. Mr. Mansel has quoted the excellent saying of Bacon, that "a cripple, if he finds the right "way, may advance further than a racer who chooses "the wrong." How many a Unitarian has confessed the force of the undogmatic, unlearned statements, of men who merely spoke what they had felt and learnt through trial and sorrow! How much more the Evangelical movement of the last century really affected the position and creed of Unitarians, than all the arguments of Horsley or of Magee! How much has the belief of a Spiritual Power acting upon men and in men, which was the belief that gave that movement its character, insensibly operated upon Unitarians, and subverted some of their most resolute denials! These observations are patent to all who have had any opportunities of studying the subject and of tracing the ecclesiastical history of the last seventy years. If they do not at once commend themselves to Oxford divines,—if it strikes them that this Evangelical movement has strengthened the Unitarian cause on one side more than it has weakened that cause on the other,—you will not be at any loss to understand this contradiction. You will think that it may be accounted for without setting aside the other evidence to which I have referred, without any retractation or modification of the inferences which I have drawn from it. On this point I wish to make a few observations which will illustrate, I hope, the whole subject, and will show how it bears upon the points which are at issue between Mr. Mansel and me.

The belief of a Spirit living and working upon men and in men, has become strangely blended with all the thought, feeling, speculation of this time, with its strongest moral convictions, with its worst fanaticism and imposture. In one shape or another the question is driven home upon us all. *A* Spirit, but *what* Spirit? There is a power acting upon us somehow and somewhere, acting upon our own very selves, acting not upon our senses, but upon us who guide the senses. May it not be an evil power as well as a good one? Can we know which it is? The Evangelical teachers who have given such a strong impulse to this belief meet this inquiry as far as they themselves and their followers are concerned. They say, the Spirit we mean, the Spirit who works in us, is a Spirit of Holiness, One who separates us from the world, One who directs our thoughts to what is divine. But they cannot meet it so far as men in general are concerned. It has been their habit to speak of the majority as essentially unspiritual,—in some sense, under the direction and government of a bad spirit, but chiefly in this sense, that he holds them in the chains of the flesh and the world; so that the definition of mankind beyond the excepted circle is, that they are sensual and mundane. No doubt it is involved in the very nature of preaching that men should be told that this ought not to be their condition; that they are very guilty in allowing it to be their condition. But it seems, nevertheless, as if this were their normal state; as if only an abnormal process could make them anything else.

Then comes the question, what it is that constitutes the difference between those who are under the influence of this Sanctifying Spirit and those who are not. There are, or ought to be, it is said, great external differences, differences in conduct, which all can recognize. But, through various causes, these outward signs may be unsatisfactory, or may be confounded with the acts and conduct of those who have not the Spirit. The differentia is faith in Jesus Christ; faith in Him, not as the Saviour of men generally, but as the Saviour of him who exercises the faith, the Saviour from his present torments of conscience and from the wrath to come. And this faith gives him a right to call upon God as his Father, to think of himself as His accepted and reconciled child.

I present this doctrine without one painful accompaniment, one injurious deduction,—as it is embraced by some of the best men and women of our times. In that form the modern Unitarian protests against it. He protests against the assumption of evil as the ground of Humanity. He protests against the limitation of spiritual operations to an excepted body. He protests against the notion that the Spirit can prompt any acts but good and benevolent acts, and that any such acts should be taken to be not spiritual. He protests against the notion that a certain belief about Christ—perhaps that any belief about Him—is necessary to make men good and benevolent, and such as God would have them be. He protests against the statement that only those who have such a faith may call God their Father. He protests against what he takes to be an invasion of the dignity and oneness of the Father. He may vary in his idea of the Christ. Sometimes He may appear to him simply as a glorious man; sometimes as invested with the goodness if not with the perfections of God; sometimes as hovering between Humanity and Divinity. But this uncertainty does not make him less but more a representative of the feelings of our time, which are characterized in all directions by a like uncertainty.

Here, then, is excuse enough for the Evangelical to say to the Unitarian of this day, 'You have accepted 'our Spiritualism in place of your old Materialism, ' that you may become more effectually our antagonist.' Here is an excuse for the Oxford Theologian to say to the Evangelical, 'See what has come of

'your indifference to Dogmatism! See what encou-
'ragement you have been giving to heresy! Do you
'not perceive the necessity of recurring to our old
'Anglican Divinity, and inculcating formulas and prac-
'tices which have nothing to do with the spiritual
'conceptions and individual apprehensions you have
'talked of so much?'

Plausible statements both; both, I think, ineffectual for any practical purpose. What is done cannot be undone. All the Oxford divines cannot cause that that Evangelical movement should not have been and should not have wrought mighty consequences. All the Oxford Theologians and all the Evangelical preachers put together, cannot hinder God's education of men from going on in His way, not in theirs. But if, leaving the Unitarians for awhile, they will seriously consider what is involved in their own confessions, and how far they are adhering to those confessions, they may become fellow-workers in that Divine education; they may address themselves courageously to minds which appear the least in harmony with their own.

The Evangelical teachers are unfairly accused of being indifferent to Dogmatic Divinity. Dogmas concerning the Fall of Man, concerning the Atonement, concerning the Trinity itself, have become an integral part of their teaching. But many understand by Dogmatic Divinity the Divinity of our Creeds. The title has always appeared to me singularly inapplicable. The Creeds emphatically proclaim Persons to our faith; Persons who reveal themselves in acts; they set forth no dogmas about Depravity, about an Atonement, about any other matter whatsoever. If the charge were that the Evangelical teacher reversed the method of the Creeds, I think it would be a tenable one. That teaching begins from a Spirit speaking to and in us, and rises gradually to a Father; the Creeds begin from the Father, and end in the announcement of a Spirit proceeding from the Father and the Son, to build up a community of Saints, to bestow Forgiveness of Sins, to quicken our mortal bodies, to give us life everlasting. This assuredly is the Theological Method. It is the method of the Bible, where all things descend from God to the creature, instead of ascending from the creature to God. Suppose, then, the Professional Theologian—the University teacher—firmly resolved to take this method for his guide, and not to abandon it for any other, however it may recommend itself to him as more formally and technically convenient; he would find himself on the same living ground with the Evangelical; he would also find himself adhering, not to the arrangements of men, but to the order of the divine Revelations. But he would be precluded from determining a number of questions which the Evangelical by his course of thought is obliged to determine. The One God the Father of all, the Maker of Heaven and Earth, would be regarded as revealing Himself in the

Only-begotten Son, Who was born of the Virgin Mary, Who suffered under Pontius Pilate, Who was crucified and dead and buried, Who descended into Hell, Who rose again from the dead, Who ascended into Heaven, Who sitteth on the right-hand of the Father, Who shall come to judge the quick and the dead. There can be no question that these are acts which connect Him with the human race, acts done and to be done for Man. Then the Spirit will indeed be believed to be the *Holy* Ghost, since none other could proceed from such a Father as Christ had manifested in His life and death. And His acts would be acknowledged as corresponding to the acts of the Son, as acts wrought in a Human Society to bind the members of it together, to emancipate them from the sins that separate them from God and from each other, to give them the full perfection of all their faculties of spirit and sense, to fit them for the fruition of God for which they are created. Such a creed assuredly explains the strong conviction of the Evangelical that all his discovery of his own evil, all his faith in a Deliverer, all his worship of a Father, is the effect of a Spirit working upon his spirit. But it does not allow him to assume for an instant that his knowledge of evil proves evil to be the law of his race; that faith is in a deliverer who is the deliverer of him and not of all mankind; that the Spirit who is teaching him to claim his rights as a member of Christ and a child of God is not leading all men to vindicate the same rights, is not convincing all of sin for not vindicating them.

Wide as such teaching is from much of that which often passes under the name of Evangelical,—from that of persons who truly deserve this honourable designation,—I am satisfied that many of these persons are craving for it, and would give thanks to God night and day if they might accept it. For then they would feel that they had a Gospel which they could preach to all people everywhere, without stint or limitation; one which they would not need to pare down or qualify lest some should accept it who had no right to it; one which could never bear any fruits but those of His Spirit. And the more earnestly the Evangelical teacher remembers what is implied in his name,—the more he demands such a Gospel, and will endure nothing that falls short of it,—the more, I am convinced, he will be led into agreement—not with me, he may regard me as the most mischievous of heretics, if he likes, but—with that old lore which he often feels to be precious, but which he as often contemplates through the mist of modern interpretations.

If I went on to say that I am equally satisfied that this same Creed is commending itself, and will commend itself more and more, to the hearts and reason of many Unitarians, I should rest the observation upon these grounds. (1) That their strongest and deepest convictions dwell in the name of Father, which in the Creed assumes its rightful prominence. (2) That many of them are impatient of that half ideal half actual Christ, which they have been compelled to substitute for the mere man of Nazareth, in whom their fathers believed, and would rejoice to substantiate the ideal, and to connect it with the actual, if they could only believe that in confessing a Son of God who was with the Father before all worlds, they were asserting more perfectly the meaning and the glory of that Father; that in confessing a Son of Man who was really born of a woman and suffered under Pontius Pilate, they were vindicating the true greatness of mankind more than all high phrases about humanity can ever vindicate it. (3) That many of them are aware of the confusion which haunts their minds, and in some measure the minds of all men in this generation, when they speak of a spirit and spiritual influences; how easily an earnest faith in these may run into Pantheism, confounding the spirit of the world with the Spirit of God; how easily it may run into self-worship, confounding the devotee with the object of his devotion: and would rejoice if they could acknowledge a living Spirit proceeding from the Father and the Son, not to glorify individual saints who are unlike the rest of their race—not to communicate sudden impulses and impressions to creatures who have no spiritual mould or constitution,—but to awaken that spirit in man which is the very sign of his kind, which distinguishes the human race from all other races; so to build up a human fellowship, capable of showing forth the character and mind of the Father in Heaven, capable of doing good works, capable of overcoming evil in itself and in the world, capable of that knowledge and life of God, after which men in all ages have been aspiring. (4) That there is a discontent in the most enlightened Unitarians of our days with the mere notion of a numerical Unity; a sense that such a Unity does not and cannot satisfy their most fervent longings; that therefore many among them may be *more* ready than those who have been ecclesiastically trained to accept that idea of a transcendent Unity—of distinct persons in one Godhead—which is implied in all our formularies, and which is expressed in the Creed that they regard with a natural aversion and horror.

For though I started from the Apostles' Creed, I have been obliged to introduce some of the principles which are more fully developed in the others, not for the condemnation of Unitarians, but for the removal of what seem to me their just objections to some of our current and popular statements. They complain, not without clear and strong evidence, of our shrinking from those words which occur in the Evangelist to whose authority we appeal most constantly, 'The Father is greater than I;' 'The Son can do 'nothing of Himself but what He seeth the Father 'do.' It is a common objection that orthodox divines make efforts to explain these words away;

that they speak of Christ as claiming an independent authority. Now if they would study the Nicene Creed, and consider how resolutely (as Bishop Bull demonstrated) it sets forth the subordination of the Son to the Father; not (so Pearson allows that the Fathers taught) merely as a man, but as a divine Person; they would not suppose that the idea of the divine Unity, which the Church holds, is inconsistent with these passages of St. John. They would rather perceive how wonderfully these passages help to unfold it; and moreover to reveal the divine Mystery as the true groundwork of human obedience and human self-denial.

And to go to the more offensive Creed. If we had been strictly mindful of the words, *Such as the Father is, such is the Son, and such is the Holy Ghost,* which we repeat in it, should we not have avoided that which is the greatest scandal of all to Unitarians; that which I believe has been most fatal to our own Theology and Morality; the habit, in scholastic lectures or in pulpit discourses, of representing the Father as having one mind towards men and the Son another; the habit of forgetting that the Spirit who seeks to make us just and true, is the guide to the knowledge of that mind? Is the Athanasian Creed so great a barrier between us and the Unitarian as this contradiction of its fundamental maxim is?

Comments which I have made on the damnatory

clauses of this Creed have led many (at one time you) to suspect me of using words in a non-natural sense. I trust I was not guilty of that great sin; if I was, may God give me repentance for it! But this I must say, that Mr. Mansel's Lectures, and the popularity they have acquired, have given a somewhat different complexion to the controversy on this question. If the doctrine that there is no faculty in men which can take cognizance of the Eternal and Absolute, is henceforth to be the only orthodox doctrine, two consequences will follow. (1) That construction of the Athanasian Creed which makes it declare that those who do not hold a certain *dogma* concerning the Trinity must without doubt perish everlastingly, will be the only admissible construction. Now many statements as I have heard respecting this Creed, I never yet found a person who said that he did himself take it in this sense. For any one must perceive that if he does, he is not merely dooming Unitarians, Arians, or Sabellians, to perdition; he is not merely dooming to perdition such men as Cyril of Jerusalem, and all others who did not accept the Homoousion; he is passing sentence on all worshipers who do not form precisely that notion of the Trinity which the terms of the Creed embody—every one who from any cause is incapable of understanding those terms. These consequences are not only so appalling, but so monstrous, that every one exclaims, 'I am sure the writer 'did not mean *that*. Such a Creed could not have 'been recited by generations of serious men, if they 'had attached that signification to it.' And therefore all have implicitly, if not explicitly, held that the faculty which forms notions and opinions is not the only one—not the great one—in our minds; that that which belongs to man, that which has an interest in the Nature of God, is altogether different from this; that a person may have an exact logical conception of the terms in the Creed, and yet divide the Substance and confound the Persons in the way which the writer of the Creed would have thought most fatal; that a person may have a most imperfect logical conception of those terms, or no conception at all, and yet may be thinking of it as the writer of the Creed, or, at all events, as the Searcher of Hearts, to whose judgment the Creed refers us, would have him think, and that he may be in the right way to learn hereafter what he knows not now.

(2) If Mr. Mansel's doctrine is the only sound one, any construction of the words 'perish everlastingly,' but that which makes them describe a future state of endless mental or physical torment, is inadmissible. For Eternity, in any sense but as an idea which is deduced from the conditions of Time, according to his teaching, cannot be an object of human thought. This notion of endless futurity has been abstracted by a natural and legitimate process from the conditions of Time. That which is associated with the idea of God has not been and cannot be so ab-

stracted. Now most of us have thought that the sentence, 'The Father is Eternal, the Son is Eternal, the 'Holy Ghost is Eternal,' fixes the adjective as having its fullest, truest, most radical meaning when it is linked to those divine Names. Learned and unlearned, layman and priest, so far as I have been able to observe, hold this conviction till some opposing opinion displaces it. And so long as they maintain it, so long no theories whatever respecting eternal punishment can prevent them from supposing that the adjective, somehow, retains its meaning in *that* application. Mr. Mansel's doctrine consecrates that notion which has been hanging about the other, and has never been able to harmonize with it, into the only possible one. That to which it has been attached must be discarded. And this, I conceive, is the great service which his work is doing and will do for Christian Theology, and for the Christian Church. We have been living in a dim twilight, not quite knowing whether we were sentencing to damnation other men for not holding a certain opinion about the Trinity, or whether we were testifying of actual Persons, of a perfect Unity—wherewith we may have fellowship, and so become partakers of Eternal Life—from which we may be divided, and so suffer that kind of death which is measured by no minutes, days, or centuries, which can be conceived under no conditions of time. For our own sake, for the sake of the Church and of the World, it is needful that we should not dwell in this twilight any longer. It makes every suspicion of our own judgments, every hesitation about judging our fellows, a step into indifference. We are afraid to confess a dimness in our mind respecting any part of the Creed we have learnt, lest we should be bringing ourselves under its penalties. We are afraid to look at the variety of opinions, to which the doctrine of the Trinity has given rise in all ages, lest we should seem to be standing on a pin's point of difference from all these opinions, and should not be able to balance ourselves on that pin's point. And so there grows up in our minds that which I have described before, and must describe again, as an orthodox Atheism—a readiness to acknowledge anything whatever about God, because we do not in our hearts confess that He lives. I have seen something of this Atheism; it has made me tremble for others and for myself; it would, I think, have driven me to despair, if I had not seen another process going on sometimes in the same persons, still oftener in persons severed by education and habit from our Church and its factions. Through severe mental struggles, through outward circumstances apparently the most unpropitious, one side after another of that Name which they have been used to connect with the refinements of controversial divinity comes out livingly before them; takes hold of them with a mighty grasp; reveals itself to them as the interpretation of a number of tormenting problems; and yet withal humbles them even more than it elevates. So have I seen—am I speaking falsely or deceiving myself?—that very idea of the Son, of His eternal generation, of His being the God of God and Light of Lights which clergymen have thought they might cast aside for some more easy, natural, less mystical form of doctrine, presenting itself to persons brought up in all Unitarian traditions, and having no secular motives for deserting them—not as an opinion which they might hold, but as a substantial verity which could give them rest and comfort amidst the reeling and rocking of all mere opinions. So have I seen these persons fastening on the faith of the Son of God being indeed very man, as the support of all that they had hoped for their kind, of all that seemed too good to be true respecting it. And I have noticed, at first with wonder, afterwards with humiliation, that the part of the mystery which lay in shadow for them still, was just that which appears to me most needful for the defence and protection of their old convictions—the belief of a Personal Holy Ghost proceeding from the Father and the Son, realizing and restoring that Unity which their distinctions might appear to interrupt. I wondered at this fact for awhile, not only because the strength of their original acknowledgment of the Oneness of God had led me to expect that they would have more quickly acquiesced in this portion of the Creed than in that which has overpowered them; but because, as I have said already, the confession of a Spiritual guide and educator appears to be in some sort a special characteristic and necessity of our age. But humiliation has taken the place of surprise, because the more I reflect, the more it appears to me that the belief of a Holy Spirit, in that sense in which the Creeds proclaim Him,—I mean of a Uniting Spirit,—must be weakened and marred, if not effaced, in the hearts of men generally, by the spectacle of a broken and discordant Church. We say that the Spirit is given to form a Communion of Spirits; all ask where it is. They see men united in the confession of an Infallible Dictator; but they find nothing in that confession which seems more than a treacherous semblance of agreement; nothing which answers to *this* idea. They see men apparently agreed in the confession of certain dogmas, but that agreement is as unlike this Communion as anything can be. They see men calling themselves spiritual and elect of God, and trying to associate on that ground; but dare these men say that this association satisfies even their conception of a divine Fellowship, to say nothing of that which the Church holds out to us?

I thank God, my dear friend, I thank God in my inmost heart, for these disappointments and discomfitures. I believe He is showing us the grounds of Unity. I believe He is making us feel how far deeper they lie than we have imagined, how far firmer they are. If we have confessed a Father of an Infinite Majesty, an honourable, true, and only Son—the discovery of a Holy Ghost, a Comforter, in whom they are One, will be to us the dawn of a new hope for the Universe, the assurance that that which appears so far off, and yet which we are all feeling after as if it were very nigh, is yet to be; and that if we are not worthy to see it, God may, through great crises and struggles, be preparing the manifestation of it for our children. The conviction that He is preparing it, and that then all which Fathers and Schoolmen have spoken of a Trinity in Unity, which man is created to behold and dwell in—will find its full justification; that the Mystery will be proved to have been about all men; that in all times, and in different ways, through their infinite perplexities, it has been revealing itself to them; that the discovery of its fullness and brightness will throw a light upon all earthly things, upon the past, the present, the future—this conviction, and not the desire to find an excuse for insulting Mr. Mansel, led me to write as I did about the Trinity, about those who hold the Creeds, and those who impugn them. He may deem what I have written very foolish and mystical, but at least it expresses thoughts which are not quite compatible with that purpose. If I might do it without offence, I would implore him, by the common blessings of our Christmas festival, at least to acquit me of that unspeakable meanness.

Very truly yours,
F. D. M.

LETTER XIII.

THE HUMAN MANIFESTATION OF MORALITY.

My dear Sir,

The pages in Mr. Mansel's 'Examination' between p. 73 and p. 90, are comments on my tenth Letter. In the course of them occurs that passage to which I have often alluded in this Sequel; that wherein he charges me with wilful falsehood. I shall give you the whole of that accusation, and the grounds of it, in the writer's own words; but I must first advert to the subject which has called it forth, and which must retain its importance, whatever becomes of my opinions or my character.

I have endeavoured to show that the observations of Kant respecting our faculties, like those of Butler, may have the greatest worth in a criticism on those faculties,—that any additions to them might, in such a criticism, have been out of place,—and yet that they may be entirely inadequate as a groundwork either for Theology or for Morality. The Conscience in each man bears witness of what is right for him to do, of what is wrong for him to do. By its very nature the Conscience does not *make* the right or the wrong. Therefore, however much Butler may have affirmed that it *has* an authority of its own, we are surely safer in saying that it *confesses* an authority; and that what it confesses must speak to it, that it may exercise its functions rightly. The Speculative Reason in men, so Kant affirmed, bears witness of an Infinite and Eternal. It falls into illusions when it tries to conceive the Infinite and Eternal; however little account, therefore, Kant may have made of a Revelation, his Reason does demand a Revelation of the Infinite and Eternal. The Practical Reason, so Kant affirmed, bears witness to an Absolute and Universal Morality. In the effort to conceive such a Morality, his practical Reason appears to contradict its own Nature; therefore here too the demand arises from the practical Reason itself for a manifestation of this Absolute and Universal Morality.

These are the principles which I wished to assert in my observations on Mr. Mansel's seventh Lecture, and which I have further developed in these Letters. What I have said respecting the Creeds in my last Letter will show you that I suppose them to be unmeaning and contradictory, unless there is some faculty in us, some faculty in man as man, which takes account of the Infinite and Eternal; one which is not merely conversant with notions and opinions and dogmas about the Infinite and Eternal. I dare not call this faculty *only* a Speculative Reason. I believe there must be a Practical Reason to receive the Revelation of a Righteous Father, a Son, and a Spirit, of a divine Unity and perfect Charity. But if we look into one portion of this Creed, we find that which appears *directly* to meet the wants of that Practical Reason, so far as that demands a transcendent and yet a human morality. He who is declared to be " the Only-begotten Son of the Father, the Light of Lights, the very God of very God, of one substance with the Father," is said to have taken upon Him our Nature, to have become actually and indeed Man. This, it seems to me, is *the Human Manifestation of Morality*. There is an exhibition of a Universal and Absolute Morality, which yet, in the fullest and most perfect sense, is the Morality of Man, the ground of all which is moral in each particular man.

This, I have always maintained, is the foundation of Christian Ethics. If there is such a manifestation as this, I can understand the words that Man is made in the Image of God; I can understand how it is possible for men to show forth that Image. This conviction has to struggle with many oppositions from different quarters as well as from myself. (1) It is opposed by all who, on any ground, deny the Union of Godhead with Manhood in Christ. (2) It is opposed by those who derive the idea of Manhood from Adam, and contemplate the Incarnation merely or chiefly as a provision to repair, for a certain portion of Men, the consequences of Adam's fall. (3) It is opposed by all who suppose Morality to be expressed most perfectly in Laws proceeding from a Divine Will; and who regard the Union of Godhead and Manhood in Christ, and the Sacrifice which followed on that Union, as means for extricating individual men from the penalties imposed by those Laws. In one of these two last classes are comprehended the most influential writers in the religious journals; those who are most ready to raise the cry of heresy against clergymen and laymen, those who can raise it most effectually. They find the first fact in the Bible to be the fall of Adam. They take it for granted that they are adhering to the teaching of the Bible when they make all anthropology, and, in a great measure, all theology, dependent upon that fact. 'Was not the first man made perfect? Did 'not he lose his perfection? Is there any mean-'ing in Redemption, except as it refers to his loss of 'virtue and of Eden? Again, did not the Law pre-'cede the Gospel? Must it not be preached to make 'the Gospel intelligible? Must not men be made to 'feel that they are exposed to all the threats and 'penalties of the Law, that they may appreciate the 'mercy which Christ has procured for them?'

These, you know well, are the commonplaces of our popular divinity. They have so strong a hold upon the religious mind of the country, that any one who adopts the method I have adopted, does so at the risk of being told that he denies the doctrine of man's depravity; that he is utterly ignorant of the necessity and nature of the Divine Atonement; that he is a Mystic, a Neo-Platonist, a German Rationalist, a Pantheist, etc. etc. etc. All these imputations Mr. Mansel, who has studied Dr. Candlish and Mr. Rigg, knows very well have been brought against me, and *precisely on this ground.*

I have been wont to combat them by alleging that if we follow the writers of the New Testament, we cannot make the event of Adam's fall the centre of our divinity, for they never give it that position. That Adam appears in them as the dying head of the race, Christ as the living head of it. That if we take St. Paul literally, we must regard the appearing of Christ in our flesh as the manifestation of that truth which had been hidden for ages and generations in God. That if we take St. John literally, we must speak of Christ as having been the Light that lightened every man before He was clothed in the garments of our humiliation. That if we adhere to the teaching of any Apostle, we must regard Christ as exhibiting in human acts that Wisdom and Righteousness of God, departures from which the Law had prohibited, and declared to involve an inevitable retribution. That what the Law could not do for men by all its terrors, this Righteousness and Wisdom manifested in a Person could effect, seeing that men beholding them in

Him, may become invested with them; seeing that men, being inspired by His Spirit, may show them forth in their lives and deeds. That this idea of the New Testament Revelation is the idea that is embodied in our Creeds, which contain no allusion to Adam, which are wholly conversant about God and Christ and the Spirit. That this is the Order of our Articles, the second being on Christ taking the nature of Man, and there being no allusion to the Fall till the ninth; the ground of Humanity being thus laid in Christ, the depravity that is naturally engendered in the offspring of Adam being treated as a departure from that standard.

Such have been my statements, which I have set in different forms of speech before rich and poor, believing that the New Testament Morality is for both, and that if these things are true, it may be available for both; but which I have sometimes pressed with especial earnestness upon members of the University of Oxford, because they study an admirable book of Greek Ethics, which will, it seems to me, be of immense value to them, if they believe that there is a great human manifestation of Morality in the Son of God and of Man; but which, if they only try to add on to it a certain special Christian morality, will merely bewilder them when they apply what they have learnt to themselves, and will cause them to treat the profane and the sacred teachers, Aristotle and St. John, with equal injustice. Bear these remarks in mind; remember that my Letter turns wholly on this idea of Christian Ethics, and then read the following extract :—

"Another passage from this Lecture, selected by "Mr. Maurice for special criticism, commences with "these words : 'God did not *create* Absolute Mo-"'rality: it is coeternal with Himself; and it were "'blasphemy to say that there ever was a time when "'God was and Goodness was not. But God did "'create the human manifestation of morality, when "'He created the moral constitution of man, and "'placed him in those circumstances by which the "'eternal principles of right and wrong are mo-"'dified in relation to this present life.' On this "Mr. Maurice actually comments as follows : ' " God "' did create the human manifestation of Morality." "' 'What, is not Christ the human manifestation of "' 'Morality? Or does Mr. Mansel mean to set "' 'aside the words of the Creed, " Not created, but "' 'begotten"? He need not be afraid that I should "' 'impeach him of heresy. Happily, I should be "' 'very little listened to if I did. And I prize those "' 'words of the Creed too much, for their positive "' 'worth, to degrade them by turning them into ex-"' 'cuses for discovering flaws in the faith of other "' 'men.'

"We have seen before, in Mr. Maurice's remarks "on Sir W. Hamilton, the exact extent to which his "' 'English reverence for Scripture' forbade him to

"make a man an offender for a word. We now see
"the exact extent to which his value for the words
"of the Creed forbids him to make use of them to
"charge his neighbour with heresy. He will not
"assert the charge; he will only insinuate it. He
"will only introduce his accusation with an 'I will
"'not;' and leave his readers to draw the desired in-
"ference for themselves. Kind and considerate cen-
"sor! How deeply grateful ought his antagonist to
"feel for this beautiful exhibition of brotherly love
"and Christian forbearance! Mr. Maurice 'prizes
"'the words of the Creed;' have we not his own
"voucher for the fact? He has also kindly given us
"an exact gauge by which we may measure the ex-
"tent to which he prizes them; for he has intimated
"pretty plainly that in his opinion a man does not
"prize them, who 'degrades them by turning them
"'into excuses for discovering flaws in the faith of
"'other men.' Let the reader then calculate exactly
"how far the above insinuation differs in point of
"truth or charity from a direct assertion; and the
"result will show exactly how far Mr. Maurice's
"method of prizing the words of the Creed differs,
"according to his own confession, from not prizing
"them at all. He prizes them just so much as to
"make them the means of indirectly hinting instead
"of openly asserting; but not enough to induce him
"to abstain altogether from an accusation which is
"utterly void of truth, and which he must have

"known to be void of truth at the moment when he
"wrote it down.

"I use these last words deliberately, regretting the
"necessity of uttering them, but with the fullest
"conviction that no other explanation is possible. I
"say that it is utterly impossible for Mr. Maurice, or
"for any person of average intelligence, to have read
"the words which he quotes from the Lecture, with-
"out seeing that the Creation there spoken of does
"not refer to Christ, but to Adam; and that 'the
"'human manifestation of morality' does not mean
"the example which Christ offers to His disciples,
"but the law manifested by that moral sense which
"is common to Christian and heathen alike. I shall
"not now enter upon the question, whether the words
"of the Creed, 'not created, but begotten,' refer to
"the Human or to the Divine Nature of Christ.
"Mr. Maurice has, I believe, a peculiar theory on
"that point; and his theory may possibly have
"blinded him to the sophistry of this portion of his
"argument. But no theory can excuse a man for
"distorting the words of an opponent to a sense
"which he must have known they were not intended
"to bear; and for founding upon that distortion an
"imputation of heresy which he must have known to
"be false and calumnious.

"It is, I repeat, with the deepest regret that I find
"myself compelled to bring a charge of this nature
"against one who has so many claims to respect

"as Mr. Maurice. Nothing short of overwhelming
"evidence would induce me to make it; nothing
"would gratify me more than to believe that this
"evidence can possibly be interpreted otherwise. I
"would gladly believe, if it were possible, that Mr.
"Maurice, with all his animosity, means to be an
"honest and honourable opponent; that he is one
"who may unintentionally misunderstand, but who
"is incapable of wilfully misrepresenting. But in
"this instance it is not possible. Let me repeat once
"more my own words, with Mr. Maurice's pretended
"interpretation of them. 'God did create the hu-
"'man manifestation of morality, *when he created
"'the moral constitution of man, and placed him in
"'those circumstances by which the eternal principles
"'of right and wrong are modified in relation to this
"'present life.*' This, says or insinuates Mr. Mau-
"rice, is a heretical statement concerning the gene-
"ration of the Son of God, who is 'not created, but
"begotten' from everlasting of the Father. If any
"reader *can* believe that, under the influence of any
"amount of prejudice or misapprehension, the words
"can honestly be supposed by any one to bear this
"construction, by all means let Mr. Maurice have the
"benefit of that belief. I for one *cannot.*"—(*Examination,* pp. 77–80.)

On this extract I will venture a few remarks.

(1.) You will remember that I transferred the whole passage, one part of which Mr. Mansel says contains a direct answer to my lie, into my own book, before I made a single comment upon it.

(2.) After giving the passage in full, with all the illustration of it which Mr. Mansel himself had given, I began my observations, not where Mr. Mansel begins his quotation from me, but thus:—

"Now here we have the most distinct assertion I "can imagine, that the Gospel does *not* explain what "was left unexplained by the law,—that the mani-"festation of Christ in the fullness of time, does *not* "remove the veil which was over the minds of men "in the old dispensation. 'God could not create "Absolute Morality,' that is admitted. I rejoice that "it is,—the Absolute Morality must be in Him, His "own Nature."—(*What is Revelation?* p. 409.)

(3.) These sentences show why I referred to the Nicene Creed. That Creed is common to Mr. Mansel and me. It sets forth in words which we both accept, One who is not created, but begotten. *Him* I take to be the human manifestation of Morality. I deny that there is *any* created manifestation of Morality. My objection therefore was not to something that Mr. Mansel did not say, and which he rightly thinks that no reader of ordinary sense could suppose him to say, but precisely to that which he did say, precisely to that which he has repeated with emphasis in his denunciation of me.

(4.) In this instance then, as in every previous one to which I have alluded, Mr. Mansel assumes, that for the pleasure of misrepresenting him, I have utterly perverted my own meaning, and destroyed the whole sequence of my Letter.

(5.) The mere fact of having quoted the Nicene Creed against him, suggested the thought to me, that I who am called a heretic by the religious world, might seem to be charging him, the popular champion of orthodoxy, with heresy, and I expressed, in the passage which followed, my sense of the ludicrousness of such a design, and at the same time of its utter inconsistency with all my own professions respecting the purpose for which the Creeds were given us. Is not that the simple, natural sense of my words?

(6.) But Mr. Mansel affirms that they must bear another sense, a hypocritical and lying sense, because he has already convicted me of using similar words in a like sense respecting Sir William Hamilton. Whether he did convict me of that sin, and by what process he sought to convict me, I have considered in a previous Letter. (See Letter VII., pp. 117–119.)

(7.) Whether on these grounds Mr. Mansel was justified in offering the greatest outrage to a clergyman which one man is able to offer to another, I leave his readers and mine to judge. He says that it caused him great regret when he felt himself obliged to write down the words which contained that outrage. I think hereafter he will perhaps regret, for his own sake, not for mine, that he ever did write them down. They have not injured me at all. I have said all that I hope I shall ever have occasion to say about them.

In the course of his remarks upon my supposed falsehood, Mr. Mansel has thrown out some words which indicate the real difference between us, that difference which affects all his thoughts of Ethics and mine, that difference which appears in what we have said about the Nature of Forgiveness, of Punishment, of the conflict between Good and Evil. He says that "the human manifestation of Morality does not "mean the example which Christ offers to His disci-"ples, but the law manifested by that moral sense "which is common to Christian and heathen alike." Several questions are raised by this distinction. The first, What *is* the example which Christ offered to His disciples? Is it *not* an example of the highest human excellence? Why is it that? The answer I should make is, Because it is the manifestation of the *Divine* excellence, of the excellence of that Nature of which the human Nature is the Image, of all that men had dreamed of as necessary to Divine perfection, of all that they had felt was demanded for their own perfection. Supposing Christ to be what the Apostle says He was, the Only-begotten of the Father, and the first-born of every creature; supposing Him to be the brightness of the Father's Glory, the express Image of His Person, and also to be the Head of every man, the true root of Humanity; then we have

not only "an example set before His disciples," either those who walked with Him upon earth, or those who have been baptized into His Name since; but we have in Him that manifestation of Morality to which "law" was pointing, "that which was mani-
"fested by that moral sense which is common to Chris-
"tian and heathen alike." By His manifestation we can estimate the preciousness of that moral sense; by it we can judge the particular exercises of this sense in different nations and ages; it will enable us to do them all justice, while we feel most their errors and deficiencies; it will give us a hope and assurance that none of the longings and aspirations after glory and immortality and eternal life which were found in men before the appearing of Christ, can have been abortive. For then the forgiveness which came forth in the cry upon the Cross will be regarded as the manifestation of that Forgiveness which had been shown to past generations of men by their Creator and Lord; it will be regarded also as the perfect fulfilment of that forgiveness which they had been most imperfectly exercising towards each other. Then the severe judgments which Christ denounced against the unrighteousness of those who held down the truth in unrighteousness,—against the hypocrisy of Scribes and Pharisees,—will be regarded as the echo of the judgments which had been going forth from the throne of God in all ages, and which shall go forth in all the ages to come, till they shall be gathered into

s

one grand and conclusive judgment. They will be regarded also as the justification and fulfilment of the imperfect judgments which had been proceeding against the like evils from the consciences of men in all times; yes, which were proceeding from the consciences of the men whom Christ sentenced at that time. Then the war with sickness and sorrow and all forms of misery which Christ carried on in His miracles, will be felt indeed to illustrate His words, "The Father worketh hitherto, and I work," and to vindicate every brave and true effort of men for the extirpation of sickness, sorrow, and misery, as prompted and inspired by Him. Then, too, all pain and anguish and death will be regarded as receiving their interpretation from His Agony and Passion and Death, that Death being the vindication of the goodness of His Father in permitting it to His Creation, and showing that there is a birth to which all its travail and groans are leading. Then that sorrow and agony and death will be taken to interpret, sanctify, and fulfil all that men have endured anywhere or in any time for truth and right. Then Christ's conflict with the Spirit of Evil and His victory will be looked at, not as a solitary event, or great exception in the world's history, but in the way that Milton did, and all preachers more or less do look at it, as a witness that God had been resisting the Evil Spirit through every one of His fighting servants; as a consummation of their struggles; as a discovery of the strength in which they had prevailed; as a pledge that the fight shall not cease till the Divine purpose has been fully accomplished.

All this appears to be involved in the Revelation of Jesus Christ, the Son of God and the Son of Man. I do not say what inferences may or may not be drawn from these principles. But certainly, if God strengthen me, I will not shrink from setting them forth as a Gospel to mankind through fear of *any* consequences that may be deduced from them. And, on the other hand, I ought not to shrink from resisting any doctrines, whencesoever they may come, and whatever popularity they may acquire, which strike at the root of these principles. Such doctrines, it seems to me, were contained in Mr. Mansel's Lectures generally, but in his seventh Lecture especially.

I. In that Lecture human Forgiveness is expressly declared to have another ground than the Divine Forgiveness; they are not of the same nature. This doctrine I contended was contrary to the idea of the Lord's Prayer;. to the express command to forgive others as God for Christ's sake has forgiven us; to the parable of the servant who would not forgive what his fellow-servant owed, as their Lord had forgiven him his debt. How does Mr. Mansel meet this objection, which seemed strong to many persons who agree with his theology far more than with mine? He says, (1) that "his argument was directed against those "persons who maintain that Christ's death cannot "be an atonement for our sins, because it is more "consistent with God's mercy to forgive freely without any atonement whatsoever." I know that it was directed against those persons; I said so; I expressed my dissent from those persons, and gave my reasons for dissenting from them. But may not a very mischievous argument be directed against a wrong opinion? That which has procured acceptance for Mr. Mansel's theory, as I said when I began my answer to him, is the notion that it is convenient for the refutation of opinions which most of us feel to be wrong. If it had not that recommendation, I should never have meddled with it. The whole of this Lecture is apparently directed against the opinion that human morality can be the measure of Divine; an opinion which I have fought against perhaps as much as Mr. Mansel has. But in opposing that notion he also strikes at the belief that Divine morality is the measure and ground of the human, which I hold to be the only deliverance from it. (2) He says of me:—"He takes texts in which Christ Himself "declares the conditions on which the forgiveness "which He has purchased will be granted to men; he "takes the assertion of the Apostle that we are forgiven "for Christ's sake: and he applies these passages to "prove that there is a 'direct and a literal opposition' "between them and the words of a writer who re- "fuses to allow that we are forgiven merely because "we repent, and not for Christ's sake at all." Respecting the first clause of this passage, I would remark that it is of great value as pointing out the hopeless contradiction into which Protestant divines must fall if they refuse to acknowledge that the human forgiveness is the image of the Divine. We assert against Romanists that the gift of God's forgiveness in Christ is free and unconditional; no works of righteousness can procure it or make us worthy of it by "congruity." Our Lord's sentence about forgiveness meets us, and we make an exception for it. The most difficult of all righteous acts must be done *before* we can receive the grace of Christ! But suppose the gift of Divine forgiveness to be that which works in us the forgiveness of our brother; suppose it is His Spirit and not ours which sheds abroad forgiveness in our hearts; *then* clearly we reject God's forgiveness when we refuse to forgive one another. I cannot be too thankful to Mr. Mansel for having supplied me with this decisive argument against his hypothesis, an argument which will have weight in quarters where mine could not reach. The sophism in the last part of the sentence must, I think, by this time, be as transparent to Mr. Mansel himself as it will be to all his readers. The 'direct opposition' did not refer to our being forgiven for Christ's sake and not as the price of our repentance (though there may be a very strong opposition between that part of St. Paul's words and the doctrine about conditions to which I have just referred), but between St. Paul's principle that our forgiveness is of the same nature with God's, and has its ground in Him, and Mr. Mansel's that ours has a different nature from God's, and has its ground merely in a sense of sinfulness. (3) He says " The " very parable to which Mr. Maurice refers, distinctly " teaches that it is our duty to forgive our brethren " because we ourselves are sinners; the prayer from " which he quotes is followed by the words, *If you* "*forgive not men their trespasses, neither will your* " *Father forgive your trespasses.* Yet Mr. Maurice " can find a direct opposition to Scripture in the as- " sertion that the sinner whose trespasses need for- " giveness is not, as a sinner, the exact image of God!" The very principle I am asserting is that man, as a sinner, is not the exact image of God, but is as unlike God as possible. Forgiveness belongs to the nature of God. What I say is, that man, 'as a sinner,' is incapable of forgiveness. Out of sin no forgiveness comes. The man who is able to forgive is able because God has, by His forgiveness, raised him out of his sin. When he is so raised, he can feel for his fellow-men, he can feel for them as sinners. In so far as he is a sinner he can feel for no one; he is without sympathy. The parable and the Lord's Prayer agree in this doctrine. Mr. Mansel cannot; I think because he has not asked himself whether the greatest human manifestation of the Divine Morality was not in the act of bearing sins. (4) I had asked whether the weakness, ignorance, and sinfulness of my nature, which were said to be the grounds of my forgiveness, did not "dispose me *not* to forgive." Mr. Mansel answers:—"This is certainly the first time I ever "heard that a man's obligation to obey a law is invali- "dated by his disposition to break it. Most moralists "would say that the very sinfulness which disposes "him not to forgive, makes it all the more his duty to "resist that sinfulness and to forgive notwithstand- "ing. Is it not a man's duty especially to resist the "temptation to which by nature he is most prone?" St. Paul discovered that it was his duty not to covet. The law told him that it was his duty. That law revealed in him all manner of covetousness. A man discovers from Mr. Mansel's teaching that it is his duty to forgive. If that teaching works any good in him, it will show him his incapacity for forgiveness. And then he will begin to ask whether the power of forgiveness must not come from the forgiving God who has blotted out his sins for Christ's sake, and called him in Christ to receive his own nature. (5) Mr. Mansel again quotes the passage from the first edition of my 'Theological Essays,' which I omitted in the second. That passage had reference to the cruel feelings of alienation which the popular religious journals have created, and are creating, between the old and the young, the parents and children in our land; leading those who have been formed in the habits of one generation to suspect those who are growing up in the other confirming the elders in a hard religious worldliness, which maintains the recollection of what was once believed, by attacking real or supposed unbelief; driving the young into indifference or a defiant Atheism. Mr. Mansel's experience at a University may not have made him acquainted with this misery; I have known too much of it to be silent respecting it. Nevertheless I suppressed the passage because I found its object had been mistaken. Mr. Mansel has revived it. He has done wisely, according to a certain standard of wisdom. The journals will hail their champion as well as their disciple. They will catch eagerly at his allusions to Socinus and Priestley. They will see that an Oxford scholar recognizes and adopts their method of crushing opponents. He will have *that* reward. Will his conscience give him another?

II. To that conscience I ventured to appeal in the same Letter on another subject. Alluding to Eternal Punishment, the Lecturer said: "It becomes us to " speak cautiously and reverently on a matter of which " God has revealed so little, and that little of so aw- " ful moment; *but if we may be permitted to criticize* " *the arguments of the opponents of this doctrine with* " *the same freedom with which they have criticized* " *the ways of God,* we may remark that the whole " apparent force of the moral objection rests upon two " purely gratuitous assumptions."—(*Bampton Lectures,* p. 221.)

These words were addressed, you will recollect, to

a very mixed audience. They were uttered in a pulpit which must give the tone to a number of pulpits in the land. I know, and you know, in what way laymen speak of the use which we make of our privilege to assail those who cannot answer us, and to fix prejudices against them in the minds of our less instructed hearers. It is an ordinary topic of complaint; none, I believe, excites so much bitter feeling against the clergy in many minds; none provokes so much scorn and ridicule in others. I was writing to theological students. For their sakes I felt that I had a right to notice what appeared to me a very aggravated instance of the kind. The 'opponents of this 'doctrine' (not some specific class of them, to whom Mr. Mansel in his 'Examination' wishes to confine the remark) were 'charged with wishing to criticize 'the ways of God.' I considered the charge unfair in in itself, and put into that form of 'hinting a fault and hesitating dislike,' which makes it especially galling. The persons I had known, who adopted this opinion, were generally very sensitive about criticisms on the character of God; generally men who had suffered bitterly, and had trembled for themselves or others lest they should sink into Atheism, before they had dared to question the popular opinion or to consider whether Scripture supported that opinion. If young preachers caught from one whom they were sure to regard as a model, the habit of taunting doubters who perhaps had more fear of God than themselves, they might do a great deal of injury before they were aware of it, and might in later years have to go through some of the processes which they had treated with scorn in their fellow-men.

Moved by all these considerations, I said "the "last clause of this sentence would be highly com-"mendable in an Old Bailey Advocate; whether it is "equally admirable as coming from a Clergyman and a "Gentleman, I leave to the author's conscience." Mr. Mansel's conscience boldly meets these words. He is sure that he did say what it behoved him to say as a Clergyman and a Gentleman; my opinion upon the subject has not, as I did not expect it to have, the least weight with him. Seeing then that I have done him no harm, and only enabled him to feel more assured of his own innocence, I am glad that I used the expressions about which I felt at first a little doubtful. For they may be read by some who *have* offended in this way, and who will be the better for them; they may come back to me when I am tempted, as I often am, to acts which befit an Old Bailey practitioner better than a Clergyman. Mr. Mansel is anxious that I shall not miss the benefit which I intended for him, and therefore breaks out in this eloquent style :—

"Mr. Maurice is doubtless a most competent person "' to decide what language is proper ' coming from a "' Clergyman and a Gentleman.' His own writings "furnish conclusive evidence of his fitness to lay

"down the law upon this point. Be it known to all
"whom it may concern, that a Clergyman and a Gen-
"tleman is on no account permitted, on pain of Mr.
"Maurice's heaviest displeasure, to speak of any
"person as 'criticizing the ways of God;' but that
"he is perfectly at liberty, on the same high autho-
"rity, to make use of any of the following expressions.
"He may say that his opponent's statements are
"'such as a heathen would use to defend the Sacri-
"'fices which he offers to a malignant power.' He
"may say that his views 'stir up all the elements of
"'strife and bitterness in the natural heart;' but
"do not 'stir the spirit to any energetic action for
"'God or man.' He may speak of his 'unsightly and
"'quite portentous imaginations;' of his 'hardest
"'and most mischievous theories.' He may charge
"his opponent with a 'confusion of our God and
"'Father with Moloch and Siva.' He may say that
"'Terms and Realities are hopelessly mingled in his
"'intellect, nay, even in his conscience.' He may
"'say that the confirmed, self-satisfied atheist is the
"'only person who can receive such tidings without
"'a protest.' And he may parody the *Te Deum*, to
"exhibit as the final result of the offensive teaching,
"'We shall praise thee, O Devil, we shall acknow-
"'ledge thee to be the lord.'"

"In culling these flowers of polemical rhetoric, it
"is not my intention merely to retaliate upon Mr.
"Maurice with a *tu quoque*. If I have really offended,

"in however slight a degree, against the laws of lite-
"rary courtesy, it is but an indifferent excuse to say
"that Mr. Maurice has committed the same offence
"more frequently and more grievously. But I am
"anxious to know myself, and to let others know,
"what we may say for the future, and what we may
"not. Mr. Maurice is my accuser; and I am natu-
"rally desirous to know the standard by which he
"judges and condemns. I have no infallible faculty
"for distinguishing between that which is and that
"which is not, '*in any matter whatsoever*,' and there-
"fore, among the rest, in the matter of polite speech.
"Mr. Maurice, who has, chooses to teach by example
"rather than by precept. The foregoing examples,
"if they do not constitute a very definite standard,
"may at least, it is hoped, serve as a step towards
"attaining one. It will at any rate be highly satis-
"factory to persons who are fond of strong language,
"to know that the rule of clerical and gentlemanly
"propriety, whatever else it may include or exclude,
"gives them full liberty to make use of any of the
"above expressions."—(*Examination*, pp. 85, 86.)

Here is a series of counter-appeals to my conscience. I am glad to accept them as such. They are proposed rather too rapidly for the reflection which they separately deserve; several of them may lose a little of their effect from having been once or twice introduced to my notice in former pages of the 'Examination.' And I cannot exactly judge of their pungency in the form in which they stand in the pages which I have just extracted, because that is *not* the form in which they stand in the books whence they are taken. I believe, if any one who should happen to possess of my 'Theological Essays' the first or second edition, or the volume 'What is Revelation?' would do me the great favour of referring to the passages which Mr. Mansel has adduced, he would be astonished at the transformation they have undergone from the simple circumstance of their appearing originally in the midst of sentences which explain what their purpose was. Not having read the first of the books which is referred to for several years, I was obliged to go through the process myself. I must not waste your time and be drawn away from my subject by leading you through the same; the examples I have given in the case of men whom Mr. Mansel admires, will have prepared you for his method of quoting from those whom he despises.

But taking the passages generally, I must answer now as I answered before. If I have imputed to any specific opponent, or to any class of opponents, notions and opinions which he or they repudiate,—or have given him or them credit for feelings, tempers, habits of mind, which are not theirs, or which they are trying to throw off,—so far I confess that I have committed a sin, which demands repentance towards God, and such amendment and satisfaction as I can make to those whom I have injured. This rule I shall construe more rigorously against myself than I should against any one else. But I do not confess it as a sin that I have denounced opinions and notions which are prevailing, and which I know to be prevailing, in English Society. I do not repent of having asked men or women to consider whether these notions are compatible with the higher and nobler faith which they are cherishing in their hearts. I do not repent of having done what in me lies to point out their inconsistency with the faith which is embodied in our public Confessions. I do not repent of having tried to show that if we believe in the Infinite and Eternal God who has made Himself known to us in the Only-Begotten Son, and who works in us by His Spirit, we may throw off the incubus of those thoughts about the future ruin of mankind which intertwine themselves so closely with the popular theory of Eternal Punishment, and which will rest with a thousand-fold weight upon those who are persuaded that we can only guess about the Eternal from the things of time.

III. The last part of this article in Mr. Mansel's 'Examination' refers to a passage in my Letter respecting the Permanence of Evil. The Bampton Lecturer appeared to me to say that the immortality of Evil was not a greater contradiction to our Reason than its existence. He might not mean what I supposed him to mean; if he did, the meaning might present itself in a light altogether different to him and to me. I felt that I was ready enough to believe in the immortality of Evil; that it was the most natural thought of all to me; that if I yielded to it, I gave up the fight with Evil together; that I could only overcome it by thinking of Him who wrestled with it to the death, and rose again from the dead; that when I did set my mind upon Him, I *could* not believe in the immortality of Evil; I must suppose that it would flee before the brightness of His manifestation and that Good alone would last for ever and ever. Such a method of reasoning will always appear ridiculous to formal logicians; it will always commend itself to fighting men. If I introduced it, I did not hope that it would find any tolerance with Mr. Mansel in the former character. I did believe, that it would not be entirely lost upon him in the latter. Nor do I give over that hope yet. He may suspect me of utter insincerity, of only resorting to 'rhetorical devices,' when I speak of my own shameful indifference to Evil. I shall not suspect him of the like insincerity. I shall believe that he feels the peril which I feel, and that he will cast the most favourite theories to the wind,—because he will have evidence that they have no substance in them,—if he discovers that they hinder him or others in that strife against Evil to which we are all called, and in which each may help the other.

Very truly yours,
F. D. M.

LETTER XIV.

THE BIBLE.

My dear Sir,

My reply to Mr. Mansel was introduced by a Series of Sermons. In those Sermons I considered what answer the Bible gave to the question, 'What is Revelation?' The Letters which followed were intended to show that the principles on which the Bible and Christianity were defended in the Bampton Lectures, struck at the idea of Revelation which presented itself in every part of the New Testament;—in the simplest records of the Gospels, in the Parables, in the Miracles, in the preaching of St. Paul, in the apostolical announcements of a future judgment.

I confined myself in these Sermons to the New Testament; for I had dwelt, in a number of previous sermons addressed to the same audience, on the narratives of the Old, and on the lessons respecting Revelation which they contain. The more simply those narratives are considered, the less one departs from the direct letter of them, the more does the purpose exhibit itself. Abraham, so we believe, was delivered from the idolatry of visible things by a revelation of the Invisible God, who was with him in his tent and family, with him when he went forth to battle, and who promised to be with his seed after him. The Covenant with his descendants was the witness, to those who acknowledged it, of a continual presence with them, of a continual protection over them and their households by an Invisible God. When the slaves in Egypt had lost their faith, they were restored again by the Revelation of the I Am to Moses. Laws issuing from a mountain on which they saw no shape; the pillar of cloud by day and of fire by night; the tabernacle which travelled through the wilderness, the manna, and the water that came from the rock, were all signs and revelations of the same present and living God; always distrusted, always proving themselves true. The signs of the Presence went on, the distrust went on. Each crisis of their history is reported by the Prophet as a day of the Lord, a discovery or revelation by an outward judgment of Him who could not be seen, but who was the same from generation to generation, always with those who were forgetting Him. The evil habits into which one age after another falls, the adulteries and murders, the priestly corruptions, the unrighteous acts of the kings, are all traced to the denial of the Unseen God; each manifestation of the evil tendencies of men brings out His Righteousness into stronger relief; is a pledge that that Righteousness will turn to Judgment. The hope of a fuller, more perfect unveiling of God, is the hope which is set before the Israelites; more and more he learns to blend that hope with the appearing of a Divine King, with the revelation of a Man who shall reign over the Gentiles, and be a refuge and glory to His people Israel. Elders and Rabbis may try to separate these promises; they cleave to each other in the mind and heart of the people. It is a king they want, a king who will come forth and deliver them from the oppressions under which they are groaning.

The New Testament opens with the birth of such a King. He is shown to be of David's lineage; he is divinely born of a woman; the Idumæan king is afraid of him; he is carried into Egypt; he grows up unknown at Nazareth. Then the message of a Kingdom of Heaven is heard. The Jews are called to turn to the Righteous Lord, just as their fathers were called by the old Prophets. They are baptized, as a sign that God remits their sins. They are bidden not to say that they have Abraham to their father, because God can of the stones raise up children to Abraham. He who is coming will gather His wheat into the garner, and burn up the chaff with unquenchable fire. All these are prophecies of a revelation or unveiling of God to His creatures. Then comes the message, " This is my beloved Son." He is anointed with the Spirit. He enters into conflict with the Spirit of Evil in the Wilderness. He carries on a conflict with that same Spirit in the bodies and souls of men. By acts and by words He proclaims a Kingdom of Heaven, a Kingdom the direct opposite of the kingdom of this world, which is established in the Cæsar; a Kingdom of Righteousness, a Kingdom working for the deliverance, not for the bondage of human creatures; a Kingdom reaching a region which that kingdom cannot reach; a Kingdom proving itself in a small sphere to be effectual for the cure of all the evils to which the flesh and the spirit of man is heir. The Kingdom is proclaimed to be that of a Father in Heaven; He who proclaims it is treated as a blasphemer by Jews because He calls Himself the Son of God. He is delivered up to the Gentiles to be crucified, because as a King He is undermining the imperial throne. He dies, He rises, He ascends on high. The Apostles on the day of Pentecost declare that by His Resurrection He has been revealed as indeed the Lord of Men and the Son of God. They say that the gift of a Spirit who is speaking by the lips of a set of poor Galileans is the sign of His filial nature and His Kingly power. By that Spirit they say He is binding together a Society of men to be witnesses of His Resurrection and divine Kingdom. He will be revealed or manifested, in their day, taking vengeance on the unrighteous city which professed to worship God, and had rejected the image of Him in Jesus of Nazareth.

In the years between that prophecy and its fulfilment, the Apostles go forth as the heralds of this Revelation to men. Others are joined with them. A Hellenistic teacher announces, more boldly than they have done, the downfall of the Temple and the disappearance of the Jewish ritual. He defends himself by tracing the continuous Revelation of a Living God to his nation, and their resistance in every age to the Holy Spirit; the greatest resistance being reserved for that Righteous One for whose coming all legislators and prophets had been preparing. He dies witnessing that the Son of Man is standing at the right-hand of God. A young man who is consenting to his death, as he goes forth to bind those who, like Stephen, are testifying that a crucified man has revealed God to men, is himself overpowered by a Revelation of that crucified man. By this name he ever after describes that which changed the purpose of his life. There was a vision to his external eye. But what he dwells upon is the unveiling of the Son of God in him; that, he says, has fitted him to be a preacher to the Gentiles. That has enabled him to tell all men that they are fellow-heirs and of the same body with the Hebrews whom he had taken to be the exclusive favourites of Heaven. Whatever Church he forms, to whatever Church he writes, it is still of the Revelation of the Son of God as the Prince and King of Men that he writes; it is still of the Revelation or Manifestation of the Spirit, who alone enables them to call Christ the Lord. He bids the Churches look for and wait for the Revelation or Manifestation of the Son of God. He says that there will be such a Revelation or Manifestation in that age.

It might be regarded as a specially Pauline phrase; so much does it penetrate all his discourses; such illustration does it receive from his experience. But if you turn to the writings of St. John, you begin to fancy that it is also specially his; so much does the idea of an unveiling or manifestation of God pervade his Gospel; so much is it the central idea of his Epistle. How name and idea both meet us in that final book of the Bible, which not only English criticism, but the most recent and adverse German criticism assigns to him, I need not remark; except for the purpose of saying, that if we gave that name its true emphasis, if we did not deprive it of the sense which it bears in every other part of the New Testament, I believe that book would be found to possess a worth which is not affected by the different theories about various passages in it, or by the different dates which are assigned to the fulfilment of its prophecies; that in the light of that name the theories might explain themselves, and each contribute something to our instruction; that in the light of that name what has been supposed to be the book of riddles might become an interpreter of the riddles which have haunted us in earlier books; that in the light of that name the fullest conviction that the Apostles were not deceived in the expectation of a Judgment and Unveiling in their own day, might be reconciled with the fullest belief that the history of Christendom has been a series of days of the Lord, and the belief that there shall be one day in which all things that are hidden shall be revealed, because it shall be a complete revelation of Him who alone brings anything within the range of our human vision now.

This is the idea of Revelation which I have derived, not from some faculty of my own which Mr. Mansel thinks that I claim, but from the Bible; taking it as it stands; trying to follow the course of its discoveries; not leaving out any part of it in obedience to the teaching of Rationalists, not changing history into allegory in compliance with the suggestion of Mystics. Such as it is, I offer it to the reflection of those who study the Bible and reverence its authority. They may find a multitude of flaws in it; they may have perceptions of the truth which have never been vouchsafed to me; if we believe that God actually has revealed Himself and is revealing Himself to His creatures, each may hope in some measure to clear away difficulties from his neighbour's path; each may desire earnestly that his own eyes may be couched, that the light may enter into them. Suppose, on the other hand, there is no human faculty which is capable of receiving a Revelation of God as God; supposing there is no perfectly clear medium in whom He may behold us and we may behold Him; supposing there is no Spirit of whom it may be believed literally and strictly that He guides into all Truth; it seems to me that we are left to the mercy of the conceits and judgments of particular men; and that the fact of our possessing a Bible does not make us at all less at their mercy, seeing that all they can do is to abstract notions and probable conclusions from it which must be modified and moulded by the tendencies of their education and the habits of their times, and which must therefore be a most fluctuating standard for that time and for themselves, to say nothing of those who come after them.

The more I read Mr. Mansel's Lectures, the more convinced I was that this must be the result of his denial that there is in man any faculty for conversing with the Infinite and the Eternal. But the conviction reached its climax when I read his final Lecture; when I found how he shrank from the examination of the actual contents of the Bible; when I perceived that he threw us back, as the ultimate result of all his inquiries, upon the evidences which show why the Bible should not be rejected; when I found him telling the students who listened to him that they were to receive the Bible as a whole or not at all; so leading many to place it on their shelves as a book which it was safe to accept without any careful study of its contents; so driving others who felt doubts about particular passages, to cast it aside altogether.* All

* Mr. Mansel complains of me because in speaking of him and those who adopt the "all or nothing" method, I supposed them to address Infidels in the words of Moses when he struck the rock, "Now, ye Rebels." I did not know that Mr. Mansel or Mr. Rogers would feel hurt at being compared to the greatest of Legislators and the meekest of men. I am very sorry. I will never do it again.

those were clear indications, I thought, that the book, *merely as such*, was taking the place in his mind of the Revelation whereof the book speaks; and so that while it was most loudly vaunted as the word of God, it was actually ceasing to be the word of God at all.

The observation of the way in which the subject of the Bible was handled in the Lecture which was devoted to that subject, led me to consider how its particular texts had been treated in the special Lectures. Mr. Chretien thinks that I ought not to have entered upon this inquiry; that the special objects of the preacher warranted him in adopting mottoes rather than investigating texts. Be it so. I may have been wrong; the object of discouraging theological students from imitating that course may have been too predominant in my mind. But I still hold that the mottoes ought to have been appropriate, and that on the whole they were singularly inappropriate. And I must say that the defence which Mr. Mansel has put forth for them, has not the last weakened, but greatly strengthened that opinion. I objected to the text, *Ye shall not add unto the word which I command you, neither shall ye diminish aught from it*, as a preface to a discussion on Rationalism and Dogmatism, because it so evidently refers to the Revelation of a Living Being, and the discussion so evidently referred to notions and opinions about this or that matter. Mr. Mansel replied:—" But surely, if we in any de-
" gree share in these privileges of the chosen people;

"if the Bible is to us the word of God, no less than
"the Law of Moses was to the children of Israel;
"there is no reason why the prohibition against add-
"ing to it or taking from it may not be as applica-
"ble to us as to them, and as liable to be trangressed
"now as then."—(*Examination*, p. 93.) I fully believe that we do share in the privileges, and in far
more than the privileges, of the chosen people; I believe that their dispensation was only a preparation for
ours. And therefore I believe that we ought not to
cast away these privileges by representing our condition as merely that of men who have a certain book
put into their hands which they may interpret in a
Dogmatic or Rationalistic sense. I believe that was
the error of the Jews, Pharisees and Sadducees, in
our Lord's time. The sense of a living Revelation
had departed from them; they took interpretations,
Rationalistic or Dogmatic, as the substitute for it.

In reference to the next of these texts he says of
me:— " His objections are based upon the point which
"separates his philosophy from mine, and turns, not
"on the meaning which the text must bear, but which
"it must bear to suit Mr. Maurice's speculations. He
"holds the Bible to be a complete revelation of the
"Infinite as Infinite. I hold it to be an adaptation
"of the Infinite to the finite capacities of men."—
(*Examination*, pp. 93, 94.) I need not tell you that
I do not hold the " Bible to be a complete Revelation
"of the Infinite as Infinite." I should hold such

words to be nonsense. I believe that the Being to whose Holiness and Goodness and Wisdom and Truth there are no limits, has perfectly revealed Himself in His Son Jesus Christ; that the Spirit of Holiness and Goodness and Wisdom and Truth dwelt in Him without measure; that His acts and life were the manifestation of the Father. I have admitted any finiteness in the incarnate Christ—the finiteness of a little child—which is compatible with this true and full revelation. I admit, and I believe the Bible admits, none which interferes with it. And I believe that we only feel a contradiction in the revelation, because we are all more or less infected by that false philosophy which supposes that Goodness and Truth are not Eternal things, which tries to apply to them the measures of time. Christ, who was always in communion with his Father, possessed them perfectly; we have a very weak grasp of them, some a weaker, some a stronger; but those unseen things which we grasp ever so feebly, are still eternal things.

In connection with these texts, the following note is introduced :—

"In his remarks on the first of these texts, Mr. "Maurice garbles the language of Scripture in a "manner which has already brought upon him the "severe animadversion of one of his reviewers. He "says (p. 470), 'If Mr. Mansel had acknowledged "'any connection between the Old and New Testa-"'ment, would not this passage have led him to that

"'in the third chapter of the Second Epistle to the
"'Corinthians, in which St. Paul contrasts the Old
"'Dispensation with the New in this very respect,
"'winding up with the memorable words, *And we
"all with open face beholding the glory of the Lord,
"are changed into the same image from glory to
"glory*'? It would scarcely be believed, without
"the witness of his own citation, that Mr. Maurice,
"while in the very act of charging his opponent with
"misinterpreting Scripture, omits from the text of
"St. Paul the very word which shows that its mean-
"ing is the direct reverse of that which he assigns to
"it:—'beholding *as in a glass* ($\kappa\alpha\tau o\pi\tau\rho\iota\zeta\acute{o}\mu\epsilon\nu o\iota$)
"'the glory of the Lord.' Was Mr. Maurice afraid
"that, if he had cited the text entire, the language
"would have recalled another passage of the same
"Apostle, in which a similar expression, 'we see
"'through a glass darkly' ($\delta\iota'$ $\dot{\epsilon}\sigma\acute{o}\pi\tau\rho ov$ $\dot{\epsilon}v$ $\alpha\dot{\iota}v\acute{\iota}\gamma\mu\alpha\tau\iota$),
"is directly contrasted with seeing 'face to face'? It
"is an unfairness similar in kind, if not quite so fla-
"grant, that Mr. Maurice speaks of St. Paul as con-
"trasting the Old Dispensation with the New *in this
"very respect;* whereas the Apostle himself expressly
"tells us that he refers, not to that passage in the
"Old Testament in which Moses is told that he can-
"not see the face of God; but to that in which it is
"said that 'the children of Israel could not stead-
"'fastly behold the face of Moses.' Yet the man who
"can do this dares to charge his opponent with emp-

"tying texts of their significance!"—(*Examination*, pp. 93, 94.)

I should have supposed that the readers of my book and of Mr. Mansel's Lectures were sufficiently familiar with their Testaments to correct any omission like that which I am charged with, and that there could not have been an act of more consummate foolishness than to venture it for the sake of establishing an argument or confuting an opponent. Whatever may be done with books which lie out of the reach of ordinary Englishmen, the English translation of St. Paul's Epistles is happily not one with which such tricks may safely be attempted. If others might afford to run the risk, does not Mr. Mansel know well enough that I of all men could not? "I have "brought on me the severe animadversion of one of "my reviewers." What, only one? The writer in the 'Literary Churchman,' to which Mr. Mansel alludes, ascertained that I had never read Anselm's Monologium or Proslogion, though I had given extracts from one, and an account of both, in the book from which I quoted a passage; but a less erudite critic might be able to prove that I had "omitted the words of St. "Paul, which show that the meaning of the text is "directly the reverse of that which I assign to it." I apprehend that Journalists in general, with the best inclination to find me out in a transgression, knew too well what the common feeling about the passage is among readers of Scripture, to think that they could raise any successful cry against me for having departed from it. In our early English versions of the passage the words 'in a glass' do not appear; Wickliff renders it: "*And alle we that with open face seen the glorie of the Lord, ben transformed into the same ymage fro clerenesse into clerenesse, as by the Spirit of the Lord.*" He, no doubt, followed the Vulgate, not connecting *speculantes* with *speculum.* "*Nos autem revelatâ facie gloriam Domini speculantes, in eandem imaginem transformamur à claritate in claritatem, tanquam à Domini Spiritu.*" Tyndale has it: "*But we all beholde the glory of the Lorde with his face open, and are chaunged into the same similitude from glory to glory, even of the Spirite of the Lorde.*" In Cranmer's, the *speculum* appears:—"*But we all beholde in a myrroure the glorie of the Lorde with his face open, and are chaunged into the same similitude from glory to glory, even as of the Spryte of the Lorde.*" It may be doubtful whether the Genevan intends the 'open face' to apply to the Object, or the beholder: I should think, to the latter: "*But we all beholde as in a myrrour the glorie of the Lord with open face, and changed into the same image from glory unto glory, as of our Lorde's Spirit.*" The Rheims loses the mirror again:—"*But wee al beholding the glorie of our Lord with face revealed, are transformed into the same image from glorie to glorie, as of our Lorde's Spirit.*"*

* I may add Luther's version, which is very remarkable:—"Nun

I do not put forth any one of these versions as better than the authorized one,—on that subject I offer no opinion,—but as helping to determine the sense which the King James Translators found in the words, the sense which I believe most of their readers have found in them. The "mirroure" is not something which impedes the view of the object, or makes the object itself less clear; it presents the object; it enables the beholder to see it truly as it is, without a veil. The other notion of the glass comes out in Bretschneider's Lexicon, but very curiously. He assumes the sacred writer to deviate from the natural, classical force of the word. These are his words:—
"Κατοπτρίζω (à κάτοπτρον, *speculum*), monstro in "speculo; repræsento aliquid tanquam in speculo. "Medium: intueor me in speculo. *Sic apud profa-* "*nos.* *Sed* 2 Cor. iii. 18 est intueor tanquam in "speculo, *i.e.* imaginem rei video quæ cognitio paulo "obscurior est, quam si rem ipsam video."* Of course he refers, as Mr. Mansel does, to the word ἔσοπ-τρον, and under that to the passage in 1 Corinthians xiii. But I would venture to ask, do the words ἐν αἰνίγματι, make no difference? Is it not in *them* that the 'darkly' lies? Why need it be in the

"aber spiegelt sich in uns allen des Herrn Klarheit mit aufgedecktem "Angesicht; und wir werden verkläret in dasselbe Bild, von einer "Klarheit zu der andern, als vom Herrn, der der Geist ist."

* Liddell and Scott say, "It suits the whole context much better to take κατοπτριζόμενοι τὴν δόξαν in the sense of REFLECTING the glory."

glass at all; except as that glass is discoloured by the eye that looks into it?

Be that as it may, the subject considered in the 13th chapter of the first Epistle, is the difference between the light which was vouchsafed to the Apostle and the Corinthians then, and the light which they might look for when they had passed out of the world. The subject in the 3rd chapter of the second Epistle is the difference between the light which was vouchsafed to them under that dispensation, and the light which the Israelites of a previous day had possessed. How can the one be used to alter the interpretation of the other? If Sir John Herschel was to speak of the little knowledge of physics which men have now compared with that which they may have a century hence, would he contradict anything he has said about the superiority of the knowledge which any in this age may possess to that which greater men possessed before the days of Kepler and Newton? Are the two statements inconsistent? Would not he who refused to recognize the advantage of the present over the past, practically deny the hope of the future? Let it be granted that St. Paul speaks of Moses coming forth with a veil on his face when he presented himself to the children of Israel. The contrast is still that Christ does not present Himself with a veil on His face; the contrast is still that we may with open face look to Him who with open face speaks to us. The contrast is still that the glory of the Lord is revealed in Him as it was not revealed in Moses; that a Communion is established between heaven and earth in the Son which could not be established in the Servant. Mr. Mansel's restless effort to avoid this acknowledgment, affords a greater help in understanding his Theology than all his subtlest arguments.*

These answers to my objections therefore bring us back to that grand debate between us, whether the Revelation is only one which it has pleased God to make, and which we cannot assume to be an actual revelation of His own very nature, or whether that Nature is the Archetype of ours, and therefore ours can only be reformed by being brought into contact with it, by contemplating it in the Mediator, by being baptized with the Spirit.

And so I may conclude this Letter, the last but one, I am thankful to say, of the series.

Very truly yours,
F. D. M.

---

* In the Postscript to my Letters I referred to the passage in the 13th chapter of the first Epistle, expressly for the purpose of contrasting St. Paul's method of opposing present to future privileges with Mr. Mansel's. I concluded that, according to him, men never could have the vision of God in any after condition, unless they ceased to be finite. Mr. Chretien has made nearly the same remark.

LETTER XV.

CONCLUSION.

My dear Sir,

The pages from 95 to 108 in Mr. Mansel's 'Examination' contain that sentence which I quoted in the first of these Letters, wherein he gathers up all his charges against my book into a denunciation of it, as nearly unparalleled in English literature for unfairness and malignity. From these evil fruits he draws an inference as to the value of the faculty, which he says that I claim to possess, for judging between the right and the wrong, the false and the true. Then he confidently asks his readers to confirm the judgment which he has pronounced against me. He proceeds, in a postscript, to speak of me as "eminently entitled to respect," and to intimate that the differences between us would probably be found very slight, if I could be induced to give up certain theories which Mr. Rigg supposes that I borrowed directly from the Neo-Platonists, which *he* rather suspects were obtained from them at secondhand.

As I have considered each of Mr. Mansel's charges separately, I am the less anxious about them when they present themselves in a heap. The passage, however, in which they are collected will be good for quotation, and will save many the trouble of going into details. Mr. Mansel, well aware as he is of his own popularity and my unpopularity, has very plausible grounds for expecting with much assurance an instant and decisive verdict against me on all the counts of his indictment. Supposing it however to be a just verdict, I do not exactly see that he will have proved that there is no faculty for pronouncing upon the right or wrong, the true or the false, in one subject or another. I should imagine that he was exercising that faculty when he passed sentence on me for flagrant outrages against honesty and truth; I should suppose he was appealing to the same faculty in his readers when he invited them to ratify his sentence.

That being a convicted liar and hypocrite I am "eminently entitled to the respect" of Mr. Mansel and his readers, is a statement which I confess myself unable to understand. I should not offer such respect to persons whom I believed to deserve those titles. I cannot accept it from those who suppose that I deserve them. Mr. Mansel may have all the courtesy which his reviewers attribute to him; but he owes something to his Order, and his courtesy should not betray him into expressing the slightest respect for one who has disgraced it. I claim an acquittal from the awful charges that have been brought against me, because I have shown that the accuser has not established any one of them. I expect that acquittal from those persons whose opinions I care for, be they ever so hostile to me. But I ask no indulgence whatever—certainly not the faintest shadow of respect—from those who hold me to be guilty.

The method of adjusting our theological differences which Mr. Mansel proposes might tempt me far more. It would be a small sacrifice for so great an end to renounce my allegiance to the Neoplatonical teachers, seeing that I have never paid them any allegiance. Bystanders are said to know more of a game than those who are engaged in it. I am not, therefore, bold enough to dispute the authority of Mr. Rigg respecting the character of my opinions. I would only observe that any expressions I have used respecting the divine and human nature of our Lord, to which he can take objection, are contained in Sermons and Lectures on the Gospel and Epistle of St. John. From that Gospel and that Epistle, and not from Plotinus, Iamblichus, Proclus, I have professed to deduce my principles. If I appealed to the Law and the Testimony, would it not have been as well for Mr. Rigg to do the same? Surely he would have confuted me more easily, and have exposed me to English readers more effectually, than by connecting me with writers of whom (perhaps to dissemble my love) I have been wont to speak rather uncivilly, and with whom all may not be so well acquainted as Mr. Rigg is.

But though nothing looks more generous than a proposal to grant me peace if I will surrender a territory to which I have never pretended that I have any right, there is a concession implied in these preliminaries which I cannot make. I have not been contending for a theory or against a theory. While Mr. Mansel is holding his wise opinions, and I my foolish ones, the world is going on; men are born into it and die in it every hour; there are things which we see that deserve our earnest thoughts, there are things we do not see that deserve more earnest thoughts still. The question I have considered in this book is whether these things which we do not see, and these things which we do see, are not of more worth than all the theories and opinions of all the Neo-Platonists and all the Scotch Philosophers in the world; and whether there is not a way in which human beings who live and die may be actually and truly acquainted with both, though they may be utterly unable to form opinions or to judge of opinions. Not the question whether I confound the Infinite and the Finite, and Mr. Mansel accurately distinguishes them, has been at issue between us; but the question whether the Infinite and Eternal God has or has not unveiled Himself to human beings, and whether, though all distinctions and the very names Finite and Infinite should be utterly dark to them, they may not dwell in His Light, and have fellowship with it, and gradually come to see all things by it. This, I believe, is the question of questions for our generation. In it are involved, as I think, these issues; whether there shall be any living Theology, or only a dry skeleton divinity, which struggling and suffering men will scorn, and which soon those who elaborate it and proclaim it will be weary of; whether there shall be any living Morality concerning all men, or only a System of Morality which shall not really concern any man; whether there shall be a living and advancing Physical Science, or only conflicts of one learned speculation against another; whether there shall be a living Politics, grounded on the acknowledgment of a permanent Order adapting itself to the changing wants of man, or only endless altercations between one political dogma and another, ending in a Tyranny in which men acquiesce, because they have tried all plans and notions and have found them barren; whether Education in our Universities shall acquire new vigour from communion with the wants of actual men, and the Education of the world be raised and purified by communion with the learning which is stored in Universities, or the knowledge of the past shall only help to rivet the prejudices of the present age, and the vicissitudes of the present to make the witness of the past as capricious as its own. If I did not feel these interests to be at stake, I might have entered on the controversy with the motives and for the ends which

Mr. Mansel attributes to me. As I do feel them to be at stake, I think I abhor such motives and ends as much as he can abhor them.

I should be doing injustice to Mr. Mansel as well as to myself if I admitted that the strife between us had been about the merits or demerits of a certain opinion. I fully acknowledge that he had a moral purpose in his Lectures, a purpose of the greatest importance for our country and our generation. I do not mean the overthrow of Hegel and the Rationalists. I have doubted always, and I doubt still, whether we are very greatly and directly interested in that result. I mean the cultivation in us of a sense of our own ignorance; an abatement of our desire to judge what is above us; an awe of the Majesty of God. His experience of young men in his own University may well have taught him how vehement and exclusive the critical spirit is in all our minds; how early it manifests itself; how very wide it is in the range of topics with which it intermeddles. He may have felt a natural and laudable wish to fix boundaries beyond which it should not pass. "Here, within the region "of the finite, criticize as you will; beyond lies a "world into which you cannot enter without being "guilty of folly as well as sin." If I have not honoured as I ought the feelings in the writer which prompted such prohibitions as these, or the feelings in his readers which responded to them, I am much to blame. I know for myself, more than for others, how much we require to hear the words continually sounding in our ears: "Take off thy shoes from thy feet; "the place whereon thou standest is holy ground." I know how much we want the trembling of the shepherd who was afraid to look upon GOD.

But the more I need help for this end,—the more I respect Mr. Mansel's desire to produce this awe,— the less do I acquiesce in the method in which he has dealt with our pride, and has sought to foster our humility. Many in whom the critical temper is very rampant, will simply despise the limits which are imposed upon it; they will say that as long as men do speak of the Infinite and Eternal, these are legitimate subjects for their comments. Some of them will accept the restrictions, because they will pronounce all that is not finite merely fantastic and imaginary. Both will continue to cherish a habit of mind which is as fatal to the right treatment of the finite as of the infinite. For is not that Criticism false which fancies that it can comprehend the purposes of a man or the functions of an insect? Is not that the right Criticism which is always aiming at the apprehension of the highest Truth and Good; so learning to appreciate all the lower forms of Truth and Good; so learning to detest and to eschew the Counterfeit and the Evil? This Criticism I know you desire to cultivate. Shall we not cultivate it, and all that awe which we need in our studies and in the acts of our lives, if we believe that the Eternal and Infinite is always near us, is always speaking to us, is always preparing us for the knowledge of His creation and Himself? Do we not begin to know anything when we cease to measure it by our own standard? Does not every lower nature —does not our own—become a worthy and profound study to us, when we look up to a higher Nature, and believe that we are intended to participate in that? Thanks be to any teacher who shows us how wonderful it is that we should be capable of such greatness! —thanks be to any teacher who tells us that men could not reach it if the most High had not stooped to their littleness! But if there is no such capacity, is not the Universe emptied of its meaning and its glory?—does not man shrink into the meanest of all the atoms which compose it?

Affectionately yours,
F. D. M.

THE END.

www.ingramcontent.com/pod-product-compliance
Lightning Source LLC
Chambersburg PA
CBHW022116230426
43672CB00008B/1402